The Path to Private Practice

- THE PATH TO -
PRIVATE PRACTICE

A ROADMAP FOR
Speech-Language Pathologists
and Occupational Therapists
Considering Private Practice

Jena H. Castro-Casbon, MS, CCC-SLP

THE PATH TO PRIVATE PRACTICE

A Roadmap for Speech-Language Pathologists and Occupational Therapists Considering Private Practice

This publication is designed to provide accurate and authoritative information in regard to the subject matter covered. It is sold with the understanding that neither the author nor the publisher is engaged in rendering legal or other professional services. While the publisher and author have used their best efforts in preparing this book, the purpose of this book is to educate and give suggestions. The authors and publisher shall have neither liability nor responsibility to any person or entity with respect to any loss or damage caused or alleged to have been caused directly or indirectly by the information contained in this book.

Printed in the United States of America

First Edition

ISBN 979-8-218-14959-8 paperback
ISBN 979-8-218-14958-1 ebook
Library of Congress Control Number: 2023902530

Cover and Interior Design by:
Chris Treccani

Created with the Book to Millions® Method

Included with your purchase of *The Path to Private Practice* are several Book Bonuses, which include:

- Worksheets
- Training videos
- Case study interviews
- Additional resources

The Path to Private Practice will walk you through the first stage of your private practice journey, which I call the Plan Your Private Practice stage.

As a former professor, I know the importance of taking action based on what you learn and that many speech-language pathologists (SLPs) and occupational therapists (OTs) identify as kinesthetic learners, people who learn by doing.

This book isn't meant to be read passively; it's meant to be underlined, written in, and experienced.

Utilizing the additional resources provided as part of your purchase will help you get the most out of this experience and set you up for success on the path to private practice.

PrivatePracticeBook.com/Resources

Download the Audiobook (Free!)

To say thank you for reading this book, I would like to give you the audiobook version 100% FREE!

I know that SLPs and OTs are busy, so being able to listen to the book while on the go will give you a better chance of finishing it.

Listen to this book on a walk, in your car, or around the house. I even narrated the book myself, so it will feel like we're having a conversation.

PrivatePracticeBook.com/Audio

Join The Start Your Private Practice Program™!

The Start Your Private Practice Program™ is the best program to help SLPs and OTs start successful private practices step-by-step—so you can have the freedom, flexibility, fulfillment, and financial independence you desire *and deserve.*

The Start Your Private Practice Program™ covers everything from legalities and marketing to billing, taxes, and more. First, we'll help you get your ducks in a row so that your private practice is built on a solid foundation. Then, we'll teach you how to find ideal clients in your area and how to bill for your services. Think of this program like the missing course from graduate school that teaches you how to start a speech or occupational therapy private practice, step-by-step. (We even provide continuing education credit!)

Most clinicians don't have the time, energy, or expertise to figure out how to start a business on their own. We've simplified the process and taken out the guesswork of starting a private practice by giving you access to on-demand training videos, checklists, worksheets, and ongoing mentorship.

There are children and adults in every community who are going without services or stuck on wait lists. Seeing clients through your private practice is a wonderful way to help your community while helping yourself, too. Join The Start Your Private Practice Program™ today so we can help you get set up and started.

Visit PrivatePracticeBook.com/Resources to learn about The Start Your Private Practice Program™ (and take advantage of a special offer for our readers!).

PrivatePracticeBook.com/Resources

Dedication

This book is dedicated to SLPs and OTs who have joined the Private Practice Movement.

You are changing the lives of your clients, their families, and your community. You're also changing your life, your family's life, and the future of your profession.

You are a Change Maker.

"Be the change you wish to see in the world."
—Mahatma Gandhi

Table of Contents

Introduction

"I just want to help people."

How many times have you said or thought that?

You chose the field of speech-language pathology (SLP) or occupational therapy (OT) because you want to help people and make a positive difference in the world. Our professions are a calling for smart and dedicated clinicians who want to help children and adults navigate challenges and live fuller and more independent lives. We are called to serve and are uniquely qualified to help people through our extensive education, training, and clinical experience. As much as we love our professions, many clinicians are frustrated with their jobs.

Two Major Problems and One Fantastic Solution

Problem 1: Clients Deserve Better Care

There are people in every community who need speech and occupational therapy but are going without services or are stuck on wait lists. When they do get therapy, it's often limited, rushed, or provided through a service delivery model that isn't ideal (e.g., mixed-group therapy). Often, people who need services don't qualify for long enough to make progress, if they qualify at all. Clients with diagnoses, disorders, and differences that warrant speech and occupational therapy aren't usually helped by quick fixes. Our clients often require ongoing treatment in order to make significant progress. School, hospital, and early intervention systems are failing our clients. Our clients deserve more help than most traditional settings provide. Savvy clients and families seek private therapy to supplement services.

Problem 2: Clinicians Deserve More

As SLPs and OTs, we long to provide high-quality clinical care without sacrificing ourselves or our families. We want to provide therapy that helps our clients make amazing progress, but we're often faced with limitations on the type and frequency of treatment we can deliver.

When you don't have full control over the care you provide, you may feel:

- Guilty that you're not able to do more for your clients
- Frustrated that school and hospital systems aren't allowing your clients to get the help they need
- Insecure regarding your clinical competence
- Worried that you're burning out

With each passing year, clinicians wonder:

- Is this the year that I'll be able to make more of a difference?
- Is this the year when administrators will finally understand what we do?
- Will the school system impose caseload or workload limits?
- Will the hospital hire more staff?
- Is this the year when I'll finally get paid more?

Year after year we work hard, suggest changes, and hope that things will get better. School and hospital systems are very hard to change. With bureaucratic and financial interests coming before client care and employee satisfaction, you're fighting a losing battle. If you can't change the system, it's time to create your own system.

SLPs and OTs are hard workers. We work tirelessly for the needs of others, but often lose sight of our own needs.

Many of us chose our profession for the sake of flexibility and a steady job, only to find that our jobs aren't nearly as flexible as we need them to be and that the pay is too steady—in other words, we rarely get raises or bonuses. As SLPs and OTs, we are overworked, overtired, and underpaid.

And it's getting worse.

School and hospital systems aren't set up for clients or clinicians to be successful.

We face expanding caseloads and high productivity requirements, and we often spend more time documenting services than delivering them.

Another common problem is not having control over how we deliver client care due to bureaucratic restrictions. Not having control over how you do your job is one of the leading causes of clinical burnout.[1] Burnout is the greatest threat to SLPs and OTs staying in these professions long-term.

Additional causes of burnout are "low emotional and intellectual stimulation at work, emotional fatigue, long hours, excessive commitment, and lack of recognition."[1] If you burn out, you can't help people.

Clients are falling further and further behind; clinicians are burning out and leaving the profession. They are running out of time, and we are running out of hope. If only there was a way to help everyone get what they need. . . .

Private Practice Is the Solution

Private practice *is the best way* to help clients get access to the care they need and for clinicians to have full control over their professional, personal, and financial lives. It's a bridge that helps clients and clinicians get what they need by providing an outside-the-box solution.

Private practice is a win-win for everyone. It's great for you, it's great for your clients, and it's great for your profession.

If Private Practice Is So Great for Clients and Clinicians, Why Aren't There More SLP and OT Private Practices?

Why aren't there more SLPs and OTs in private practice, especially when private practice is so popular in other health professions (e.g., psychology, physical therapy, social work, etc.)? I've considered this question, and I think the answer comes down to three things:

1. SLPs and OTs don't learn about private practice in graduate school.
2. There are a lot of myths and assumptions about private practice—often perpetuated by people who aren't in private practice.
3. People are concerned about leaving the safety of their jobs as they transition from employee to entrepreneur.

You probably didn't learn about private practice in graduate school, so it's not your fault you don't know how to start a private practice. The good news is that just like you learned the clinical skills necessary to become a clinician, you can learn the business skills necessary to be a private practitioner.

IN GRADUATE SCHOOL YOU LEARN HOW TO *be* A CLINICIAN BUT NOT HOW TO *earn* AS ONE.

JENA H. CASTRO-CASBON, MS CCC-SLP

People wrongly assume that you need $5,000–$10,000 to start a private practice, that you need 20+ years of experience, an expensive brick-and-mortar space, and so forth. *You can start your practice that way*, but I consider that the Old Way to do it. In Chapter 2, I'll teach you the New Way to start a private practice—it's much faster, cheaper, and simpler than you may realize.

You can start a part-time private practice as a side hustle while continuing your full-time job; this allows you to keep your steady income and benefits. I don't want anyone to forego income or insurance; that's why it's important to build up your practice to the point where you can safely leave your job *before* shifting into full-time private practice.

Most SLPs and OTs have full-time jobs and are too busy to figure out how to start a private practice. If you have a full-time job and a family, you're busy! Starting a private practice requires a lot of steps, and it can feel very overwhelming to figure it out on your own. The good news is that you don't have to.

My life's work is to simplify the process of starting and growing successful private practices. I've helped tens of thousands of SLPs and OTs get started, and I am happy to help you too!

Private practice takes work, and it's not for everyone. As with any other business start-up, you have to be willing to invest time and money up front in order to have more time and money later. Until recently, there hasn't been an easy path to private practice for SLPs and OTs. I am on a mission to change this.

My mission is to help at least a thousand SLPs and OTs build successful private practices each year, because more practices mean more services for the children and adults who need services.

Starting your own private practice will allow you to be the answer to someone's prayers (maybe even your own!). It will also allow you to be the change that you want to see in your life, your clients' lives, and in your profession.

Private Practice Isn't What It Used to Be

Starting a private practice isn't as difficult, expensive, or time-consuming as most people think.

Gone are the days of having to quit your job and leap into private practice without a safety net. Now there are ways to see private clients without giving up your health insurance and steady pay. There are ways to find ideal clients without spending any money on marketing. There are step-by-step plans that you can follow and mentorship that you can take advantage of to make the process of building a private practice much simpler.

It's completely normal to be excited and nervous at the beginning of your private practice journey. You're in the right place, and I'm glad you're here!

You got into this profession to make a difference in the lives of your clients, and you're a true helping- people person at heart. If you've felt unable to help your clients the way they need help, keep reading, because this book has the power to change your life. You want so much for others—but it's okay to want more for yourself and your family, too. This book will show you how private practice can be a vehicle to help you get what you need and be a hero to your clients, your community, your family, and even yourself.

If you've been waiting for a hero to come and save you from bureaucracy and bad administrators, stop waiting! Be the hero of your own story. Your future self is waiting for you to find your courage and start your private practice.

I think of private practice as a journey with several distinct stages. In each stage, you'll focus on specific goals, work through various challenges, and achieve milestones in order to move to the next stage.

Because the needs at each level vary so much, you need information and support as you make progress in the private practice journey.

Let's talk about each stage so you'll know what to expect.

Stage 1: Plan Your Private Practice

In the Plan stage, you dream about your future private practice and decide what it will look like, who you'll serve, and how you'll help them. The major milestone in this stage occurs when you decide to start working with private clients. *The Path to Private Practice* (this book!) will lead you through the Plan Your Private Practice stage.

Stage 2: Start Your Private Practice

In the Start stage, you get all your ducks in a row and create a solid legal foundation to build your private practice on. The major milestone in this stage is getting your first client. You'll start working with private clients and build a small caseload, usually on the side while continuing at your job. At this stage, it's important to know which foundational steps to complete (and in what order) and to learn how to market your practice and bill for your services. We help SLPs and OTs start their practices step-by-step with ongoing support in The Start Your Private Practice Program™.

Stage 3: Grow Your Private Practice

In the Grow stage, you start to expand your caseload and go all in on your practice. During this stage, you increase your income and impact by serving more people in your community. Your practice spreads by word of mouth and takes off. Major milestones in this stage are filling your caseload, replacing or doubling or tripling your previous salary, and hiring your first team members. When private practitioners guess their way to growth, they can end up in what I call "the Messy Middle." The Start stage is fairly linear, but you can grow in infinite ways. Getting support for growing your client base, expanding your income, setting up systems, and hiring is imperative to your success. We help private practitioners set up and follow a Private Practice Growth Plan in The Grow Your Private Practice Program.

Stage 4: Scale Your Private Practice

In the Scale stage, you expand your impact beyond your community by focusing on multidisciplinary hires, having a multilocation practice, and becoming recognized regionally, nationally, or internationally. In addition to scaling services at their practices, many Scalers write books, create courses, or engage in public speaking to help more people than they can through their practices. When you reach the Scale stage, you're mostly out of the day to day; your focus is working ON the business instead of working IN the business. You're focused on leadership, company values, financial projections, and truly being the CEO of your business and your life. We support private practitioners in this stage in The Scale Your Private Practice Program.

4 Stages of the Private Practice Journey

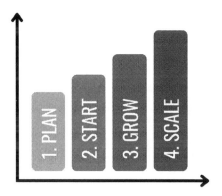

1. PLAN
2. START
3. GROW
4. SCALE

Have you ever looked at a map and seen a "You Are Here" sign? When it comes to the private practice journey, it's important to know where you are, where you're going, and what to expect from each stage.

Which stage are you in right now? _____

Which stage will you need help with next? _____

Why I Wrote This Book

This book was written for two types of people:

- Clinicians who are committed to starting a private practice and want help navigating the private practice journey
- Clinicians who are curious about private practice and want to know the ins and outs before getting started

You may be wondering if you have what it takes to be a private practitioner. If so, this book will help you realize that you're more capable than you think. After working with thousands of SLPs and OTs through every stage of the private practice journey, I have an insider's perspective on what works, and I intend to share as much as I can in this book.

You deserve more!

You deserve to be paid according to your education and experience. You deserve to have time with your family without the workday bleeding into family time. You also deserve a lunch break.

Private practice helps everyone get what they want. Your clients deserve more!

Your clients deserve access to the services they need without being stuck on wait lists or going without therapy. Your clients deserve the right amount and type of therapy to help them make progress. Your clients deserve clinicians who are able to provide appropriate care without limitations.

I decided to write this book for three reasons.

Reason #1: To Impart Business Knowledge (in a Non-Boring Way)

I've been a private practice consultant since 2008 and have helped thousands of SLPs and OTs start, grow, and scale successful private practices. This book is a distillation of everything I've learned in my years of helping private practitioners start the private practice journey off on the right foot.

The Path to Private Practice is designed to be an easy-to-read (and implement!) book for SLPs and OTs who are interested in private practice and are ready to start their journey. You love to learn, and you've spent so much time (and money) on clinical education in order to be a better clinician. Now it's time to spend time (and money) on business education in order to become a successful business owner.

There are plenty of opportunities to obtain clinical education units (CEUs) after graduate school, but there are minimal opportunities to obtain business education. I'm proud to be filling this gaping hole by offering business education programs specifically designed for SLPs and OTs who are in private practice.

You don't have time to figure out how to start and grow a business on your own, nor do you have time to sift through information that doesn't apply to you. Let me help you speed up the process of acquiring business skills so that you can do what you do best: help people.

Reason #2: To Inspire Your Dreams

I wrote this book to inspire you to build a private practice that's perfect for you, your family, and your community.

Your private practice can be:
- Full-time or part-time
- Dedicated to kids, adults, or both
- Generalist or specialist
- In-person or telepractice
- Private pay or insurance-based
- Mobile or a brick-and-mortar clinic

There is no such thing as a perfect private practice; only one that's perfect for you. Throughout this book, I'll introduce you to successful private practitioners who were once "regular" SLPs and OTs with the same hopes, dreams, and fears as you. There aren't enough SLP and OT private practice role models, so I can't wait to introduce you to people that you can aspire to be like. Their success is proof of what's possible for you. Let their stories inspire you to make your private practice dreams a reality.

Reason #3: To Invite You to Join the Private Practice Movement

At the end of this book, I'll invite you to join me and thousands of fellow SLPs and OTs who have already joined the Private Practice Movement. You may feel limited in terms of the care you can provide and the life you can live while working in traditional settings. I invite you to work outside the box by starting your own private practice.

You won't be alone. More and more SLPs and OTs are joining us every day, because they're tired of being overworked and underpaid, and they want to provide better care for their clients outside the confines of school and hospital systems. Private practice can be lonely, but it doesn't have to be. I was lucky to have mentors who helped me start my journey. Now, I'm happy to mentor you and serve as your guide.

I made a lot of mistakes when I was starting my private practice—mistakes I can help you avoid. But first, a warning:

Private practice isn't for everybody. It's not for people looking for a magic solution or a get-rich-quick scheme. It's for people who want to work hard so they can play hard. If private practice were easy street, everyone would do it.

By the end of this book I want you to:
- Choose if private practice is right for you (if it's not, pass this book on to a friend!)
- Know where to go if you want our help in implementing what you've learned (and save time and money in the process)

Trust the timing of your life.

JENA H. CASTRO-CASBON, MS CCC-SLP

It is an honor and a privilege to guide your transformation from overworked, overtired, and underpaid "regular" clinician to balanced, fulfilled, and successful private practitioner.

There is a reason you're reading this book right now.

What Is a Private Practitioner?

"If you don't build your dream someone else will hire you to help build theirs."
—Tony Gaskins

Private practice (noun): An independently owned business that provides clinical services outside the control of a larger institution (such as a school or hospital).

Clinicians choose to become private practitioners for more control over their professional, personal, and financial lives. Clients choose to hire private practitioners so that they can have greater access to services outside the limitations of traditional settings.

Private practitioners are clinicians who start their own private therapy businesses to work (and earn!) outside the box. We're tired of bureaucracy and limitations interfering with the care we can provide our clients. We're tired of dealing with high caseloads, high productivity requirements, and low pay. We're tired of working within systems that aren't set up for us or our clients to be successful—so we're creating our own systems.

We're diverse and represent all ages, races, ethnicities, orientations, genders, backgrounds, and clinical interests. We practice in big cities and small towns. We're changing the future of our profession and paving the way for greater access to clinical services. We are skilled clinicians who know our worth and aren't ashamed to charge for our services. We were made for more and we deserve more. We are proud private practitioners.

Meet Your Private Practice Mentor, Jena

I always thought I would start a private practice one day, but I never dreamed that I would start at age 26.

Only two years into being an SLP, I was feeling overwhelmed and unsatisfied and questioned whether I should stay in the profession. All I wanted to do was help people. Instead, I felt ineffective and stuck, and I worried that I was headed toward burnout.

One day, everything changed.

It was a Friday, at the end of a tough week. Two of my favorite patients were being discharged due to insurance limitations. Another pointless staff meeting went long, and I left frustrated with the administrators for making yet another decision that benefited the hospital more than my patients. I was behind on paperwork (again), and just wanted it to be the weekend. Two of my coworkers and I were eating lunch in a tiny office at the hospital where we worked. It was one of those rare lunches where you talk about things other than work. As we started to eat, my coworkers began talking about their private practices. To be honest, I had no idea that they each had a small private practice. I felt like a fly on the wall, hearing them talk. I knew they worked part-time at the hospital with me, but I didn't think about what they might be doing when they weren't working with me.

As it turned out, they both had successful part-time private practices serving just a few clients a week. I was dumbfounded. I had no clue it could work that way.

I started asking them a million questions, and light bulbs kept going off one by one. It turns out, they didn't have clinic space; they saw clients in the clients' homes. They explained that they could have office space, but it was easier and cheaper not to. I had no idea that was an option! I always assumed that being in private practice meant you had to have a clinic space with a waiting room and a receptionist answering phones and handing out clipboards. I had heard people talk about private practices with clinics having a lot of overhead. I didn't know what that meant, but it sounded expensive. I loved finding out that I could have a successful practice without having a physical clinic space.

Then they said something else that surprised me.

They were private pay only. Neither one of them took insurance. They were paid on the day of their sessions, and people willingly paid for their services. I asked if it was lucrative—and they both nodded and smiled. One of them mentioned that they made more money in a few hours of private practice than they did during the entire week at the hospital. I wasn't all about the money, and neither were they—but it was intriguing to realize that it was possible to cut out the middleman.

I realized that they were making significantly more money in less time.

I asked why they stayed on at the hospital, and they gave two different answers. One of them was a single woman who stayed on as a part-time employee for the benefits. She was earning significantly more in her practice and planned to leave in the next year, now that she could afford her own insurance plan. But in the meantime, she had exponentially increased her earnings and boosted her savings and retirement accounts.

The other person, who was very social, said he stayed for the relationships and connections at the hospital. His private practice allowed him to have deeper connections with private clients, but his part- time job at the hospital maintained his professional connections. I thought that it was cool that both of them had successful private practices that helped them earn more money without giving up the things they valued. Both had the option to leave—but had chosen to stay for the time being. I was also surprised to learn that they started when they were in their 20s— my age, at the time. That really shifted my perspective. I always assumed that you had to be in the field for several decades before starting a private practice.

I couldn't believe what I was hearing. Everything I had thought about private practice was out the window. It was a life-altering moment for me. That day, I realized that there is no one way to have a private practice. My vision of waiting to be an older SLP so that I had enough experience and money to have a brick-and-mortar location with a waiting room was shattered. I saw possibility and opportunity to break out of what was expected and follow a different path.

Jena's Path to Private Practice

Here's what my path to private practice looked like:

JENA'S PATH TO
Private Practice

I started off stuck and frustrated, unhappy with the limitations on my ability to give good client care (sound familiar?). Then, something cool happened. One of my two colleagues who had private practices said, "Have you ever been asked to treat someone privately?" I thought about it—yes, I had been asked, but I always referred whoever asked to someone else—never thinking that I could treat them myself. My colleagues encouraged me to say yes the next time someone asked if I saw private clients.

A few weeks went by. I was eagerly anticipating another opportunity to treat a private client. Then, one day, I was asked, "Do you see private clients?" This was my moment. My heart was racing. I was a mix of excited and scared and . . . I freaked out and said, "No."

The request was for a child with language delays, which isn't my area of expertise. I was disappointed and felt like I had let myself and my mentors down. A few weeks later, a friend of mine from graduate school asked if I could treat a man with aphasia. I spoke with his wife and got all the information about her husband and felt like I could truly help them. I told them my rate without allowing my voice to quiver. "Perfect," she said. "When can you start? And can you come twice a week?" This was it! My first client was scheduled! I couldn't believe it. I was so happy to be moving forward on my private practice journey.

EVERY PRIVATE PRACTICE STARTS WITH *one* CLIENT.

JENA H. CASTRO-CASBON, MS CCC-SLP

Every private practice starts with *one* client. Mine did, and yours will too.

Can you imagine having your own clients to treat? And conducting two sessions per week . . . or five or ten, twenty, or thirty? Can you imagine the feeling of working for yourself, being your own boss, having the freedom and flexibility you crave, and taking control of your life and income?

When I started working with private clients, I felt alive and reinvigorated. My job satisfaction soared when I was working for a great boss: me. Burnout disappeared, and I loved being an SLP again. I was doing meaningful work and getting paid for it. My private clients were benefiting as well. We weren't limited to a set number of sessions or specific treatment approaches. They knew that I was 100% focused on them in our sessions, which allowed me to do my best work. My clients made amazing progress and were grateful for the opportunity to work with me outside the limitations of a traditional setting. Private practice was a win for them and for me.

I grew my caseload, left my job, and never looked back. I never would have started working with private clients without the support of those two amazing mentors who believed in me more than I believed in myself. They helped me get things lined up so I could get started with my first client. Their generosity left a lasting impression on me, and I knew that as soon as I was ready to mentor others on the private practice journey, I would commit to doing so.

Founding The Independent Clinician™

I'm not sure about you, but I didn't learn anything about private practice in graduate school. My coworkers helped get me started, but after that, I had to figure out everything else on my own. When I began my private practice, the few blog posts and resources available on private practice frightened and overwhelmed me and left me feeling incompetent and terrified of making mistakes.

Why? Because everything I read focused on brick-and-mortar clinics, hiring, and getting thousands of dollars in loans for start-up costs. If I was scared, I bet everyone else was too! And the content was mostly focused on what NOT to do instead of sharing the easiest and best way to get started. They made private practice seem so scary and hard—like they were trying to scare people off instead of encouraging them.

Through my mentors, I discovered a New Way to be in private practice, which was easier and less scary than what I had read about. Why was no one teaching folks how to get started this way?

Once I was up and running, my friends from graduate school kept asking me how I had started my private practice, so I shared with them what I did. I realized that other SLPs and OTs could benefit from step-by-step instructions on how to start a private practice, so I turned my experience (and mistakes!) into resources and founded an online education company called the Independent Clinician.

I started creating and selling easy-to-follow, step-by-step resources, books, courses, group coaching programs, and retreats specifically for SLPs and OTs in private practice. I didn't want folks to be overwhelmed (like I was in the beginning), go without essential information, or waste time and money on expensive Master's in Business Administration (MBA) programs that don't apply to SLPs and OTs. I decided to price my programs like graduate level courses, because they're the missing course we never had.

Common Topics in MBA Programs[2]	Topics in The Start Your Private Practice Program™
Supply Chain Management	Pick a Name for Your Private Practice
Organizational Behavior	How to Find Private Pay Clients
Operations Management	How to Bill Insurance, Medicare, and Medicaid
Negotiation	How to Create a Private Practice Website
Business Analytics	Social Media Marketing for SLPs and OTs
Global Strategic Management	Don't Miss Tax Deductions for Private Practitioners

In my programs, I teach students the New Way to start a private practice. It's simpler, less overwhelming, and more profitable than the Old Way—which is why it works much better for most SLPs and OTs.Since 2008, I have helped tens of thousands of SLPs and OTs build private practices full-time or on the side so they can have more freedom, flexibility, and financial abundance and live an amazing life. Now I want to help you, too.

I went from being burned out and considering leaving my work as an SLP to being fired up about private practice and how it can change the lives of both clinicians and clients.

You can start a successful private practice:

- Without quitting your job
- Without waiting for twenty years
- Without having thousands in savings or going into debt
- Without a business background

. . . and this book will show you how.

Private practice is one of the best ways to live the life you've imagined. It's possible to work part-time hours and have a six-figure private practice—just like Samantha Asher, MA, CCC-SLP, who you'll meet later. If you're burned out and thinking about leaving your profession, you owe it to yourself to try private practice first.

Some people are called to join the Peace Corps, become nuns, or save whales. My calling is to help SLPs and OTs be successful in private practice. Before I lay out the steps to starting a private practice, let's talk about how to use this book so that you can start your private practice journey off on the right foot.

Four Ways to Get the Most Out of This *Book*

This book isn't meant to be read passively. This book is intended to be actively experienced. There's a huge difference between those two options, so let me explain what I mean.

The Path to Private Practice was created as an interactive resource to help you plan your private practice (Stage 1 of the private practice journey). The more you use this book and the accompanying Book Bonuses as tools to guide you, the more prepared you'll be to start a private practice.

You won't just hear from me; you'll also read case studies from regular SLPs and OTs who have become successful private practitioners.

If they can do it, you can do it, too.

Read *It*

Whether you've always been curious about private practice or an opportunity has just come up and you're scrambling to learn everything you can, read this book cover to cover to learn as much as you can about private practice and the major mistakes to avoid. Think of this book as a gift you're giving yourself. You help so many others. The information in this book has the power to be life-changing for you, your family, and your community—but you need to take action.

Write In *It*

As you read the book, underline your takeaways, scribble notes in the margin, complete the prompts at the end of each section, and make your first decisions as a private practitioner. Take notes, and then take action. In addition, you have free access to special Book Bonuses—additional activities, worksheets, trainings, and case study videos that will further enrich your experience with this book— visit PrivatePracticeBook.com/Resources.

Dream *It*

Dreaming about a new future for yourself and your family is fun! The book leads you through a series of exercises to help you start picturing the private practice of your dreams and prepare you to make it happen. My grandmother always said, "You have to dream it first." I can't wait to help you make your dreams a reality.

Share *It*

After you've read it, share the book with people in your life who will be supporting you on your private practice journey. Share it with your partner, your parents, your siblings, or your best friend. It will help them understand your private practice and learn how they can support you.

Now, Do *It!*

This book will give you enough knowledge and confidence to decide if private practice is right for you. If you follow the steps outlined in the book, you'll soon have a plan for your private practice and be ready to start. If private practice is your next step, you'll be ready to move forward to Stage 2: Start Your Private Practice.

If you decide that private practice isn't for you, you won't waste any additional time or energy on it. Either way, you owe it to yourself, your family, and your community to explore the possibility of private practice.

Ready?

Get a pen and your beverage of choice, and let's start your private practice journey together.

Chapter 1:
Why SLPs and OTs Are Joining
The Private Practice Movement

SLPs and OTs have hearts of gold and get tremendous fulfillment from helping people. Clinically, we strive to gain as much knowledge and experience as possible to serve our clients. The problem is that in most job settings, there are restrictions on who and how we can help. For example, in some school districts, in order to qualify for services, students must score at least 1.5 standard deviations below the mean or below the seventh percentile to qualify for therapy.[1] Kids who qualify don't necessarily get the frequency or quality of therapy they need. Kids who don't qualify for services are often left in a wait- and-see situation where their progress is left to chance instead of intervention. As a clinician, it feels terrible to know that people are going without services, but schools and hospitals are often so understaffed that there's nothing an individual clinician can do to help.

Another common complaint from clinicians is that we spend more time documenting services than delivering them. We also spend a lot of time in meetings that don't pertain to us. All we want to do is spend our time treating clients and helping them get better.

The SLP and OT professions frequently appear on "Best Jobs" lists.[2] Yet many of us are unhappy.

When you first started your career, I bet you were pretty happy. You were fresh out of graduate school and excited to be getting paid to work instead of paying to work in your clinical placements. But as time went on, you realized that the salary wasn't going to change much and that there were limited opportunities to advance your career. If your salary doesn't increase much over time but your expenses do, that's a problem. You want to earn enough money to do fun things like start a family, travel, or buy a house—but none of these things seem possible with your current earnings.

This isn't a rosy picture. You love your clients and your profession, but you love yourself and your family, too. There's got to be something better, right?

There is. Private practice allows you to help people on your own time and in your own way.

The Private Practice *Movement*

JOIN THE PRIVATE PRACTICE MOVEMENT

Private practice has gained enough popularity and momentum to have become a movement. A movement is a group of people with a shared purpose who create change together.

The Private Practice Movement is made up of clinicians who are dedicated to improving the lives of their clients by providing access to services outside of traditional settings. We believe that clients deserve access to better care and that clinicians deserve to have more control of their lives. The Private Practice Movement is changing the lives shaping the future of our professions.

The Private Practice Movement is bringing together over-worked, overtired, and underpaid SLPs and OTs who want to increase their impact and income by creating a new professional and personal life for themselves. SLPs and OTs are leaving traditional work settings and entering private practice to create jobs that they love and that allow them to live the life they've imagined.

In the past, setting up a private practice was a hush-hush thing, something you navigated alone. Now, there's a community of SLPs and OTs who are on this journey together. We recognize the importance of connecting with other private practitioners for support, guidance, and learning. It can be lonely to start a private practice, *but it doesn't have to be.*

Nearly half of all psychologists are in private practice (44.7%).[3] Psychologists have long enjoyed the benefits of private practice. My goal is to make private practice as popular a setting for SLPs and OTs as it is for psychologists. It's surprising to meet a psychologist that isn't in private practice. The situation ought to be the same for SLPs and OTs, but it's not.

Very few SLP or OT graduate programs teach about private practice or even discuss it. Most graduate programs only talk about traditional settings, such as schools, hospitals, and early intervention.

Professors have been known to discourage students from private practice, claiming that it's too much work or rudely insinuating that someone isn't qualified for private practice. Clinicians need to know their options, and private practice is a great option, especially if you want professional and personal freedom.

IF YOU CAN'T FIND A JOB YOU LIKE, *create one that you love.*

JENA H. CASTRO-CASBON, MS CCC-SLP

You got into this profession to make a difference. If you're not able to make a difference in your current setting, you can:

- Stay put and hope it gets better.
- Change jobs and hope it gets better.
- Create your own job and make it better.

If you want to take control of your professional, personal, and financial future, join the Private Practice Movement!

Top Reasons Why SLPs and OTs Choose Private *Practice*

More SLPs and OTs are pursuing private practice because they want to be able to take care of their clients without sacrificing themselves and their families. Balance is crucial if you want to have life satisfaction and stay in your profession long-term without getting burned out.

We are no longer willing to accept high caseloads and unfair productivity standards. We're tired of endless paperwork and required attendance at meetings that don't matter. We're no longer willing to settle for compensation that doesn't match our level of expertise or how hard we work.

SLPs and OTs are pulled in many directions. When I ask SLPs and OTs why they're pursuing private practice, seven common themes come up over and over again. Conveniently, they all start with the letter F.

I call these "Jena's Favorite F Words."

As you read this chapter, I want you to identify *your* favorite F words.

Freedom: Take Back Your Professional and Personal *Freedom*

"I just want to help people."

Have you ever caught yourself saying this? Maybe you've said it when you've been limited in how you can help your clients.

Freedom is the ability to make choices on behalf of yourself and/or your clients.

As SLPs and OTs, we have master's degrees (or higher) in most clinical settings, but administrators limit how we can serve clients. All we want is the ability to help clients to the best of our abilities. We have extensive evidence-based clinical knowledge of diagnostic and treatment approaches that we can use to serve our clients. When we're not allowed to serve people according to our expertise, our clinical freedom is limited.

When I worked in a skilled nursing facility, I faced tremendous pressure to treat patients who didn't need SLP services. After a few months, I left that position because I didn't want someone else making clinical decisions on my behalf, especially unethical ones.

SLPs and OTs know what it's like to face limitations in terms of personal freedom, too—like limitations on how and when they can use time off, whether they can use sick time to care for loved ones, and whether they have time for lunch breaks. Clinicians want to be trusted to make autonomous decisions. One of the most common sentiments I hear from clinicians who are leaving regular jobs to pursue private practice is, "I want to be my own boss." What they're saying is, "I want the ability to make my own clinical and personal decisions."

I recently asked a group of private practitioners in The Start Your Private Practice Program™ to list things that they are able to do now that they have private practices and are their own boss.

22 Things You Can Do When You're Your Own Boss (Circle your favorites!)

1. I have freedom to recommend services that I feel are appropriate with no one second-guessing or overruling me; I have the freedom to deliver my services any way I choose!
2. I can control my workload as I pass through different seasons of life.
3. I can go to my son's Halloween party without taking a half day or more to cover one hour of time off.
4. I can pick up my kids from school!
5. I can get my stress under control.
6. I can take off every holiday I dang well please.
7. I work for the best boss—myself.
8. I can leave in the middle of the day to put the Crock-Pot on, transfer a load of laundry, and run an errand!
9. I can take more than one vacation a year.
10. I can stay home with my children when they're sick without having to worry about my boss harassing me to come to work anyway!
11. I can give myself time between clients so that I can clean up or prep or maybe even use the bathroom!

12. I can give myself permission to NOT have 8 a.m. clients.
13. I can work when it works best for me.
14. I can tell everyone, "Peace out. I'm going to Tuscany to drink wine, and then I'm going to London for two weeks. See you when I get back!"
15. I can go to a fitness class at noon with no guilt.
16. I can finally get paid what I'm worth so that I can work fewer hours and slow my life down.
17. I can say no to work I don't want.
18. I don't have to explain my productivity.
19. I can say "No" without anyone asking me, "Why not?"
20. I can take on clients based on my skills, not because I have to take them on.
21. I can give myself a raise.
22. I have freedom to do what I want when and how I want to do it. It may not always be perfect, but it's always from my heart!

As you read through the list, I'll bet you were nodding along and saying, "YES! That is exactly the kind of freedom I want!"

The best way to be your own boss is to start your own private practice. Then, you'll have the freedom to make decisions on behalf of your clients and yourself. Having control over your professional and personal life (freedom) is extremely important. When you get to the end of this chapter, fill out the Balance Builder worksheet to rate the amount of freedom you have right now.

THE BEST BOSS FOR YOU IS *you.*

JENA H. CASTRO-CASBON, MS CCC-SLP

Do you want more freedom? ☐ Yes ☐ No

What would more freedom allow you to do?

_____

_____

_____

_____

_____

_____

Flexibility: Create a Flexible Schedule for Yourself and Your *Family*

"The field of speech-language pathology/occupational therapy offers a lot of flexibility."—any article featuring SLP or OT on a "Best Jobs" list

One of the top reasons SLPs and OTs choose their professions is for flexibility.

Although our *fields* have a lot of flexibility in terms of who you get to help (e.g., kids or adults, assorted disorders and differences), our *jobs* have very little flexibility in terms of our schedules.

Many SLPs and OTs seek flexible schedules because they have busy family lives outside of work. Even if you don't have children, having a flexible schedule is important in order to make time for self- care, hobbies, and so forth. Today's clinicians are seeking more balance, and having a flexible schedule is a big part of that. A career without balance leads to burnout.

Traditional job settings for SLPs and OTs offer different levels of flexibility. They often appear to be more flexible on the surface than they are once you're in them.

- **Schools** follow school hours (although planning, paperwork, and report writing often happen at night and on the weekends) and have summers off (although many clinicians work during the summer).
- **Hospitals** have good benefits (although vacation time is hard to come by).
- **Early intervention** gives you the ability to schedule your own clients (but productivity requirements and low pay mean you have to do a lot of sessions).
- **University clinics** follow the college calendar, but most instructors work during the summer and between semesters, and grading and student support are more time-consuming than most people think.

When you work for someone else, they are in control of your schedule, not you. When you're self- employed, you get to make the decisions. Creating a schedule that allows for more balance is a great decision.

Private practice gives you more flexibility:

- You have complete control over your time—you set your own hours. If you don't want to start working until 10 a.m. or if you don't want to work Fridays, you don't have to.
- You can schedule your day around family priorities like dropping off and picking up children and self-care activities.
- You can build in time for documentation and billing during your workday (although many private practitioners admit to doing work at home until they can afford to hire administrative support).

Just because you have a private practice doesn't automatically mean you'll have flexibility. It's normal to have less flexibility when you first start your practice and for your start-up days to be a busy season in your life. The trick is to make sure you build in flexibility as soon as possible and keep your boundaries strong so that you don't accidentally slip into bad habits.

Have you ever sent an email that said, "I need to stay home with my son who is sick today," and then worried about the pushback that you'd get? Or worried about how staying home would impact your coworkers or clients?

One of our Start Your Private Practice students posted in our private student group that when her son was sick, she was able to stay home with him. She contacted her private clients and didn't feel guilty about canceling because she went into private practice to have more flexibility. She loved having flexibility when she needed it.

I've also had people tell me that they started private practices because they were recovering from medical issues or navigating grief and needed a flexible schedule to get through those tough times. Private practice isn't just a job setting—it's a vehicle to have more time for yourself and your family.

IF HAVING A MORE FLEXIBLE SCHEDULE IS IMPORTANT TO YOU, BUILD A JOB THAT WILL ALLOW FOR IT.

JENA H. CASTRO**IN, MS CCC-SLP

Is having more flexibility important to you? ☐Yes ☐No

What would having more flexibility allow you to do?

_____

_____

_____

_____

_____

Fulfillment: Increase Your Professional *Fulfillment*

I packed up my bag and felt a wave of excitement. It was 5 p.m. on the dot, and I was heading down the hall with a skip in my step. As I walked out the door, the air hit my face, and I smiled.

I was free.

I walked to my car, turned on the engine, and backed up. As I exited the garage, I rolled down the windows and cranked up the radio.

I was on the way to a private client's house. Suddenly it didn't matter that I had had a lousy day at work. It was after hours and I was working for myself in a way that gave me career and life satisfaction again. I was my own boss—even if it was only for a few hours a week because my private practice was still part-time. I was grateful that I had decided to pursue private practice on the side.

Fulfillment is the feeling that you're making a difference, the feeling of satisfaction with your life and/or work. Because SLPs and OTs choose their professions in order to help people, they feel a tremendous sense of fulfillment when they know that they've made a difference in someone's life. This is what drives them.

After the session with my private client, I walked down their driveway, beaming ear to ear. It was a great session. Not only did I feel it, but I could tell that he felt it, too.

I got back in the car and kept singing as I thought about my job at the hospital. I had a dream job that I was supposed to love, but I didn't. Given the time and money I had invested in graduate school, I didn't want to become so burned out that I left the field. I knew I had to save myself and create the kind of career fulfillment that initially drew me into the field.

As I pulled into my driveway, I was singing my heart out.

No one was going to stop me from career fulfillment. When I was with clients in private therapy sessions, I felt alive and free of the confines placed on me by my employer. I got to make clinical decisions that served my client. I was making a difference. I was fulfilled. I was happy. And I wanted more.

In private practice, you can have more fulfillment by:

- Going deeper with clients and making a big impact versus working a high caseload and not being sure if you're making any impact—going deep versus going wide
- Working with ideal clients in the way they need and providing quality services
- Choosing what you want to specialize in and seeing populations that are fulfilling to you (e.g., coaching parents, helping kids with sensory needs, or helping adults with swallowing issues)

I have had multiple students in my programs say that private practice brought back their spark, their love of their profession.

If you need your spark back, listen to Episode #166 of the Private Practice Success Stories podcast— "'Private Practice Gave Me My Spark Back' and Other True Confessions of Start Your Private Practice Students." Visit PrivatePracticeBook.com/Resources to listen to this episode and download our podcast playlist.

PRIVATE PRACTICE ALLOWS YOU TO GO DEEPER WITH A SMALLER NUMBER OF CLIENTS AND *have a big impact.*

JENA H. CASTRO-CASBON, MS CCC-SLP

Do you want more fulfillment? ☐ Yes ☐ No

What would having more fulfillment mean for you?

_____

_____

_____

_____

_____

_____

Finances: Achieve Financial *Independence*

In the previous section, we talked about fulfillment. Although fulfillment is necessary for career satisfaction, *fulfillment doesn't pay the bills.* If you've got bills to pay and mouths to feed, seeing private clients is a great way to earn more money.

Financial independence is the ability to comfortably pay your expenses and still have money left over. We didn't go into the SLP and OT professions for the money, but we don't want to be struggling financially, either. We have advanced degrees, and we're skilled clinicians! We should be financially rewarded for that.

The SLP and OT fields offer good jobs with steady pay. Although SLP and OT salaries vary according to job setting, geographic area, and years of experience, they generally range from $55,000 to $80,000 per year. Depending on your lifestyle and expenses, your salary may not be enough for you and your family. Between student loans, rising housing costs, children, saving for retirement, and wanting to have fun every now and then, the average salary doesn't go as far as it used to. In most traditional clinical settings, if you want to earn more money, the only way to do it is to wait for annual 2%–3% raises. We aren't compensated more for working harder. Some might argue that when we're more efficient, our employers give us more to do. (Sigh.)

Many school-based clinicians are paid according to a salary schedule. In order to increase your salary in most school settings, you have to pay in time (waiting years to earn more until you hit a salary cap) or by completing additional coursework (which may not be directly applicable to your profession).

Here are five ways that school clinicians can earn more:
1. Move into administrative positions (most clinicians don't want to be administrators).
2. Keep working (it takes decades to reach maximum earnings; then, your income is capped and you can't earn more).
3. Gain more professional education (often paying out of pocket; some districts may pay for courses that don't necessarily pertain to your field).

4. Move to a different district (not everyone wants to move, and sometimes you drop down the career ladder by moving).
5. Take up stipend work (but many school clinicians choose to work in schools because they get the summers off).

School clinicians literally have to pay to earn more money. School pay scales serve school districts, not clinicians. Pay increases are slow and salaries are capped.

If you're a school clinician who has already worked your way up several rungs of the career ladder or is set to earn a pension, it may be hard to leave. In fact, it may not be financially smart to leave altogether; you should probably stick to seeing private clients on the side. In such cases, you have to do the math to figure out what's best for you. Don't leave a job if it doesn't make financial sense to leave.

Ever heard the phrase "cut out the middle man"? Your employer is the middle man. They are making money off of your work and only giving you a percentage. This is true for all employers. It's not necessarily a bad thing—businesses need money to continue to grow. The problem is that some companies chronically underpay their staff and don't reward hard work or loyalty.

Here's the truth: You can't be financially independent if someone else has control over your earning potential.

If you have the desire to earn more, seeing private clients full-time or on the side is a great way to supplement or replace your income without getting any more degrees. You already paid (or are still paying) for your clinical training; why not use your expertise to help more people while earning more money?

In private practice you are paid per client, not based on case-load. This gives you full control over your earning potential, which is incredibly liberating.

No more waiting for raises.

No more slow climb up the pay scale. No more cap on what you can earn.

You can literally give yourself a raise overnight by taking on more clients or increasing your rate. And because you can earn more money in less time (e.g., $125 per hour versus $45 per hour), you don't have to work as many hours in order to make the same or more than you earn at your day job.

Clinicians aren't usually trying to increase their income to buy sports cars or frivolous high-ticket items. They want to be able to:

- Pay for loans, weddings, kids, mortgages, retirement, and fun stuff
- Earn what they're worth and be in charge of their rates and raises
- Make more while working less
- Afford nicer things
- Choose to only do work they're paid fairly for
- Donate to charities
- Sponsor local sports, such as tee ball teams

I am passionate about women taking control of their financial futures. I want you to earn more money so that you can do good things for yourself, your family, and your community. Seeing private clients is an excellent way to earn more money.

Sometimes people get nervous when I talk about money, because they associate wanting more money with greed or other negative words. If earning more money has this kind of negative connotation for you, substitute the word *finances*. The word *finances* implies responsibility.

Having more money amplifies who you already are. If you're a kind and generous person, you'll be able to be even more kind and generous when you have more money.

Early on, one of my private practice mentors told me, "It's dangerous for anyone—but particularly for women—to rely on one income stream." She was a living example of someone who was committed to building multiple streams of income.

At the time, she:

- Had a part-time job at the hospital where we both worked
- Had a small but successful private practice
- Taught fitness classes multiple times per week
- Consulted with school systems regarding augmentative and alternative communication
- Owned a two-family home and rented out one side of it
- Invested in the stock market

She taught me several lessons that reshaped my life and career.

First, she taught me that it's not greedy or selfish to want to earn additional money. Earning more money is financially responsible for your family and allows you to be more generous to others.

Second, she opened my eyes to the option of creating multiple streams of income and not being just an SLP. She saw something in me that I didn't see in myself—the capacity to become an entrepreneur and help more people than I was helping at the hospital. Before our conversation, I had a very narrow view of what I could do with my degree. Afterward, I realized that I didn't have to be pigeonholed into working for others for the rest of my life.

Because she selflessly taught me how to start a private practice—a private practice that was somewhat in conflict with her own—I learned how to have an abundance mindset, knowing that there are plenty of clients to go around. She also modeled mentorship, which encouraged me to mentor fellow clinicians and even start a company that allows me to do this on a large scale.

Had we never met or had she not been generous with her advice:

- The Independent Clinician™ wouldn't exist.
- This book wouldn't exist.
- The Start Your Private Practice Program™ and The Grow Your Private Practice Program wouldn't exist.
- My abundance mindset and commitment to helping SLPs and OTs see additional opportunities and possibilities might not exist.

If you want more from your profession and your life, you have to be willing to go get it. You have the power to create more income in your life, but you have to do the work to make it happen. It's worth it, trust me. You can do it. My mentors believed in me, and I believe in you.

Case Study
Meet Bobbi Adams-Brown, M.A., CCC-SLP, B.S. Elem. Ed.

Bobbi is an SLP who I met in 2017. She contacted me because she was interested in working with private clients as a side hustle, but she had school loans and thought she should pay them off first. I suggested that earning more money would provide her with the means to pay off her debt sooner, and that's exactly what she did. Bobbi started seeing private clients on the side and selling digital therapy materials, which gave her extra money toward her loans and built up her emergency fund. Instead of waiting to become debt-free before starting her practice, she used her additional income to pay off most of her debt.

Bobbi is an alum of The Start Your Private Practice Program™ and now serves as a mentor for the program.

MONEY DOESN'T HAVE TO BE YOUR PRIMARY DRIVER.

BUT IF YOU'VE GOT BILLS TO PAY AND MOUTHS TO FEED, YOU NEED TO *earn more* THAN YOU ARE RIGHT NOW.

JENA H. CASTRO-CASBON, MS CCC-SLP

Do you want more financial independence? ☐Yes ☐No

What would having more financial independence mean for you and your family?

_____

_____

_____

_____

_____

In the Book Bonuses, you have access to the Private Practice Income Calculator, a tool that allows you to run the numbers and see what is financially possible for you and your family through private practice, even if you just take on a handful of clients. I created this custom calculator for students in The Start Your Private Practice Program, but I'm happy to share it with you, completely free. To access it, visit PrivatePracticeBook.com/Resources.

Family and Friends: Gain More Time for Family and *Friends*

Time is our most precious resource.

If you want to spend more time with your family and friends, you have to create a work schedule that will allow you to do so. Many SLPs and OTs choose these fields to have more time with their families, but work responsibilities (e.g., writing reports, planning, etc.) often extend beyond paid hours and bleed into family time. Commuting time adds to long hours. To a certain extent, working outside of work hours is normal, but if this practice is left unchecked, it can lead to resentment and frustration with your employer.

In private practice, you can create a flexible schedule that allows you to put the needs of you family first.

For example, when you are in private practice, you can:

- Drop off and pick up your kids from school.
- Attend all your kids' school events.
- Stay home with sick children as needed.

Of course, this freedom doesn't just apply to caring for children. I've known many private practitioners who have started private practices in order to have the flexibility to care for parents, friends, siblings, and other family members.

Case Study
Meet Kelsey Martin, M.S., CCC-SLP

Kelsey is an SLP and the owner of Playful Communication in Waxhaw, North Carolina. She specializes in serving the pediatric population and particularly enjoys working with children from birth to five years old. She keeps her private practice small deliberately, because this allows her to be with her children and show up for all of life's moments with them! Having her own private practice has allowed her to shift from being work-focused to being family-focused.

Kelsey is an alum of The Start Your Private Practice Program™ and The Grow Your Private Practice Program.

To hear Kelsey's full story, listen to the Private Practice Success Stories podcast, Episode #120, "Staying Small on Purpose." Visit PrivatePractice-Book.com/Resources to listen to this episode and download our podcast playlist.

If you find yourself putting off private practice until your kids are older, stop waiting. Starting a private practice now will give you more flexibility to be present with your family. Waiting until your kids are older means you'll miss out on their younger years. *You can let your kids be the excuse, or you can let them be the reason.*

Are your family and friends one of the reasons you're pursuing private practice? ☐Yes ☐No

What would having more time with family and friends allow you to do?

_____

_____

_____

_____

Fun: Have More Time and Money for *Fun*

Fun is the ability to engage in activities that are exciting (or restful) during nonwork time.

SLPs and OTs love to have fun. One problem is that because we work such long hours, it's hard to find enough time for fun. Another problem is that although there are plenty of free ways to have fun, there are even more options for fun that cost money—and you may not have extra income for those things.

Sometimes, we forego taking time off to have fun because we feel guilty about being away from our clients. More than half of Americans don't take all their paid vacation time.[4] We need to have the time and money to prioritize fun!

Case Study
Meet Tracy Droege, OTR, MS

Tracy is an occupational therapist in Temple, Texas, and the owner of Rise Center. She is also an "amateur semipro tennis player" and mom. Tracy has a private practice career and plays competitive tennis. She is succeeding at both. She has literally built fun into her schedule, which is fantastic and inspirational.

Tracy is an alum of The Grow Your Private Practice Program.

To hear Tracy's full story, listen to the Private Practice Success Stories podcast, Episode #180, "Building a Private Practice For Flexibility (Including Time for Tennis)." Visit PrivatePracticeBook.com/Resources to listen to this episode and download our podcast playlist.

"You can't put a price on fun; it's always priceless."
—Stanley Victor

If you want to have more fun in your life, you need to create time (and money!) for fun. Sometimes fun just happens, but more often you have to plan for it (e.g., going on vacation with your family).

Do you want to have more time and money for fun in your life? □Yes □No

What kinds of fun things do you want to be able to do?

_____

_____

_____

_____

_____

_____

Future: Take Control of Your *Future*

The last of my favorite F words is *future*, which is less tangible and harder to define than the other theme areas because it asks you to consider two questions:

1. Do you feel like you're in control of your future?
2. Are you hopeful about your future?

SLPs and OTs tend to dream about a more positive future for themselves and their families. They dream of a future where they will have more:

- Freedom
- Flexibility
- Fulfillment
- Financial independence
- Family
- Fun

The problem is that most SLPs and OTs don't have control over their futures—their employers do. As an employee, whether you have more clinical freedom comes down to what you're allowed to do at work in terms of service delivery. Having a more flexible schedule is determined by administrators, who may or may not allow you to adjust your hours. Earning more money comes down to the organization's budget, salary schedule, or your supervisor approving a raise. Not having control of your future can lead to frustration, resentment, and burnout.

The only way to take full control of your future is through private practice. You can create a work schedule that works for you and your family now and adjust it in the future. You can choose which types of clients you see so that you feel fulfilled now and throughout your career. You can earn more money now so that you have more money and can even retire early if you want to. It's time to take your future into your own hands.

Don't wait for opportunities. Create them.

JENA H. CASTRO-CASBON, MS CCC-SLP

Do you want to have full control over your future?   ☐Yes ☐No

What do you want your future to be like?

_____

_____

_____

_____

_____

Jena's Favorite F Words

FREEDOM & FLEXIBILITY & FULFILLMENT & FINANCES & FAMILY & FUN & FUTURE

The Balance Builder

Now that you know my favorite F words, I hope that you've also identified your favorites and which ones you're striving to have more of in your life. For example, you may be longing for more flexibility and financial independence if your current employer has you working long hours for minimal pay.

A few years ago, I participated in a program for business owners. The leader facilitated a workshop using the Wheel of Life, a popular tool used in coaching and self-help. It was originally created by Paul

J. Meyer in the 1960s to help people realize their goals and discover aspects of their lives that felt unbalanced.

In preparation for this book, I decided to create a tool inspired by the original, which I call the Balance Builder. This version is specifically for clinicians and incorporates my favorite F words. If one of the reasons you're pursuing private practice is to have more balance, you'll love using this tool as a way to identify areas in which you need more balance so that you can make a plan to increase it.

> Print two blank copies of the Balance Builder, or save the PDF and open it on a device. The download is available in the Book Bonuses, which are available at PrivatePracticeBook.com/Resources.

The Balance *Builder*

Fill out a paper or digital copy of the Balance Builder.

On the wheel, there are seven preselected theme areas and one additional area where you can write in one of your priorities (e.g., free time, fitness, etc.). In addition to the theme areas, there are numbers.

Rate your satisfaction on a scale from 1–10, where 1 = not satisfied at all, and 10 = fully satisfied. Then, using a marker or highlighter, color in the theme areas so that you can clearly see which areas you've identified as having more or less balance. Once you're finished, look at the wheel and consider your life balance. Take time to reflect on the results, and think about what changes you may need to make in your professional, personal, and financial life in order to have more balance.

Ask yourself questions like these:
- In which areas do I have the most satisfaction?
- In which areas do I have the least satisfaction?
- Which results surprise me the most?
- How can I keep areas with high satisfaction high?
- What am I going to do about areas with low satisfaction?
- Can a single action improve one area?

Identify action steps to make positive changes in your life. Make sure to fill in the date of completion and revisit this exercise again in a few months after you've made some changes. After you complete it, send me a DM on Instagram (@Independentclinician) and share your reflections.

Balance over *Burnout*

It's very hard to create balance and be satisfied with all areas of your life in a traditional job, because other people are in charge of your schedule, paperwork, caseload, and so forth. Private practice is the only way to have full control over your time. So, if you're the kind of person who values balance, time with your family, career fulfillment, financial independence, and more, keep reading. In the next chapter, we'll get into the New Way to start a private practice. The New Way emphasizes balance over burnout as you take control of your future.

The first time I completed an exercise like the Balance Builder, it was part of a business coaching program I had invested in. I was absolutely horrified by the results, because they indicated how out of balance my life was. But instead of getting depressed and staying upset, I decided to make positive changes and use it as a wake-up call to prioritize time with my family. If you complete the Balance Builder and are upset about the results, you're not alone. Many other SLPs and OTs are also feeling out of balance. Don't stay upset; use the information to transform your life for the better.

If you start a private practice, your life balance and satisfaction won't immediately be in alignment. You still have to work to achieve balance and satisfaction. Setting boundaries is very important. I know lots of private practitioners who have balance because they set boundaries.

Case Study
Meet Olivia Rhoades, MA, CCC-SLP

Olivia purposefully leaves her work laptop at her clinic so that she won't be tempted to do work during family time. During her time in The Grow Your Private Practice Program, Olivia wrote a haiku about how private practice has changed her life:

Making more money.   Only working when I want.
More fun. Less stress. Win!

I am so happy that Olivia was able to achieve this, and I know that you can achieve it, too. Olivia is an alum of The Grow Your Private Practice Program.

To hear Olivia's full story, listen to the Private Practice Success Stories podcast, Episode #170, "Going All In and Growing Fast." Visit PrivatePractice-Book.com/Resources to listen to this episode and download our podcast playlist.

If you burn out, you can't help people, and you may even leave the field. If you leave the field, you've wasted all the money and time you spent earning your degree and working in the field. That's why I believe in balance over burnout.

Chapter 2:
The New Way to Start a Private Practice

When you think of a stereotypical private practice, what comes to mind?

Do you think of brick-and-mortar clinics with waiting rooms, clipboards, and employees? That's exactly what I used to picture when I thought about private practice.

Why? Because those are the types of private practices people see.

Private practices don't become successful enough to have all the bells and whistles overnight. It takes time and dedication to grow a practice from nothing into something. Having a large private practice with a bustling waiting room in a large clinic space may be your goal, but it's not how you'll start.

There are a lot of ways to be in private practice.

The majority of students in my paid programs are focused on building traditional, full-time, brick-and- mortar private practices, but others are building "lifestyle" private practices—that is, they're creating businesses that serve their lifestyles and schedules.

Megan Ramirez, MS, CCC-SLP, is an American with a private practice based in Argentina. She sees her clients via telepractice. She designed her schedule to not start until late morning (in keeping with Argentine tradition), and she enjoys three-day weekends. Megan sees clients in several states and across different time zones so that she's always available during the most popular times.

Ashtyn Mouton, MEd, CCC-SLP, is an SLP in Orlando, Florida, who started her private practice while on maternity leave. She wanted to make sure that she was able to have a flexible schedule for her daughter while providing financially for her family. She built her private practice to have enough time to balance family, clients, and self-care.

Marcia Church, MA, CCC-SLP, is an SLP in Dallas, Texas. She owns a pediatric speech and language practice and also offers individualized education plan (IEP) consultations and parent coaching. She is a former school SLP who has lived in many places. She chose to start a private practice in order to have more control over her professional, personal, and financial life. Marcia wants to be available when her children get home from school, and she's built her practice with boundaries in place to allow her to do so.

These individuals are part of a new generation of private practitioners who are creating businesses that serve both their clients and their own lives. In this chapter, you'll learn more about the New Way to start a private practice and how you can use it to create a life that you love.

THERE IS A NEW GENERATION OF PRIVATE PRACTITIONERS WHO CHOOSE THIS SETTING TO *create a life they love.*

JENA H. CASTRO-CASBON, MS CCC-SLP

Podcast Episodes

Megan Ramirez, MS, CCC-SLP, is an alum of The Grow Your Private Practice Program. To hear Megan's full story, listen to the Private Practice Success Stories podcast, Episode #192, "Cutting Out the Middleman and Seeing Her Own Private Clients ... from Argentina."

Ashtyn Mouton, MEd, CCC-SLP, is an alum of The Start Your Private Practice Program™. To hear Ashtyn's full story, listen to the Private Practice Success Stories podcast, Episode #165, "Starting a Private Practice on Maternity Leave."

Marcia Church, MA, CCC-SLP, is an alum of The Grow Your Private Practice Program. To hear Marcia's full story, listen to the Private Practice Success Stories podcast, Episode #188, "Attracting Ideal Clients to Your Practice."

Visit PrivatePracticeBook.com/Resources to listen to these episodes and download our podcast playlist.

How to Start a Private Practice without Quitting Your *Job*

The Old Way to start a private practice is to quit your job and leap into full-time private practice.

In my opinion, this is very risky. What if you realize that you don't like private practice after you've quit your job? What if you take on a bunch of debt but don't have paying clients yet?

I started my private practice the New Way by seeing clients on the side. This is actually very common. According to research done by the American Speech-Language-Hearing Association (ASHA), 64% of private practitioners work part-time.[1]

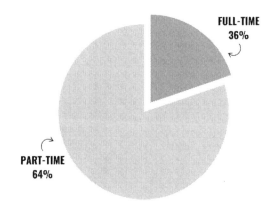

MOST PRIVATE PRACTIONERS
WORK PART-TIME

FULL-TIME
36%

PART-TIME
64%

2015 ASHA Health Care Survey

When you structure your private practice so that you're working part-time, you can see clients after work, on weekends, or over the summer. You keep the steady income and benefits from your full-time job and take your private practice full-time when you're financially ready. This gives you time to grow your caseload, your confidence, and your income while you adjust to being a business owner. It also allows you to make sure you like private practice before you commit to going all in.

Case Study
Ruth Maldonado MS, CCC-SLP

Ruth Maldonado is a bilingual SLP in California who started seeing private clients on the side while staying on at her job as a school-based speech-language pathologist. She offers bilingual evaluations and therapy for an underserved population. Within a year of starting her practice, she left her job in the schools and transitioned to full-time private practice. How cool is that?

Ruth is an alum of The Start Your Private Practice Program™.

To hear Ruth's full story, listen to the Private Practice Success Stories podcast, Episode #125, "Bilingual SLP Starts a Part-Time Pediatric Private Practice with Ruth Marquez Maldonado." Visit PrivatePracticeBook.com/Resources to listen to this episode and download our podcast playlist.

If you're concerned about health insurance and benefits, you have several options. You don't need to get insurance from an employer or a spouse. You can:

1. Keep your job with its health insurance benefits until you've grown your private practice to the point where you can afford to pay for insurance on your own.
2. See clients part-time and get insurance from a part-time employer.
3. Get your own insurance through an insurance broker, the Health Insurance Marketplace®,[2] or health-share programs.

YOU DON'T HAVE TO QUIT YOUR JOB TO START A PRIVATE PRACTICE. YOU CAN START "ON THE SIDE" UNTIL YOU'RE READY *to go full-time.*

JENA H. CASTRO-CASBON, MS CCC-SLP

Decision Time

Are you going to start your private practice part-time or full-time?

☐ Start part-time
☐ Start full-time

How to Start a Private Practice at Any *Age*

"The best time to plant a tree was 20 years ago. The second best time is now."
—Chinese proverb

I started my private practice decades before I planned to.

There are a lot of myths about private practice. One big myth is that you have to wait until the end of your career to start a private practice. I think this is based on the image people have when they think of private practitioners. They usually think of people in their late 40s or 50s, probably because that's how old the guest speaker was in graduate school.

When younger private practitioners start to think about private practice, they start comparing themselves to older people, which makes them second guess their ability to start a business and sparks insecurities about being taken seriously. There are also older clinicians who have treated thousands of clients but didn't start private practices when they were younger because they were waiting to be experts.

You can start your private practice when you have something to bring to the table.

The Old Way to start a private practice is to wait until you have "enough" experience. The SLP and OT fields are vast, and there's a lot to know. If you wait to be an expert, you may never start.

The New Way is to start young and gain experience as you go. As long as you have valuable skills to offer, you can start a private practice. You don't have to be twenty years out of graduate school to be competent and confident in your skills! In private practice, you're providing the same services you provide at your regular job—you're just doing it for yourself instead of for an employer.

Time is our most precious resource. How do you want to spend yours?

Common Excuses for Not Seeing Private *Clients*

*"If you're serious about changing your life, you'll find a way.
If you're not, you'll find an excuse."*
—Jen Sincero

"I'm Too *Young*"

If you're a new graduate and want to beef up your clinical knowledge and skills, do more continuing education. Get certified in evidence-based areas of clinical care that are in demand, areas that families are seeking out and physicians are referring their clients for.

> ### Pro Tip
> When you have a private practice, clinical and business-related continuing education programs (like mine) are tax deductible as business expenses.

"I'm Too *Old*"

You can start later in life and continue your career on your terms. You have a lot to offer! Think of all the experience you've accrued over your career. Families are willing to pay for that experience. If you're not ready for your career to be over, extend it through private practice so that you have control over your time and earnings.

"It's Not the Right *Time*"

The truth is, the timing will never be perfect; you'll never feel completely ready. Your best bet is to arm yourself with resources and know that you'll gain confidence and experience after you start your private practice. A woman was considering The Start Your Private Practice Program™. Her husband asked, "How many more signs do you need to realize that this is what you're supposed to do?" She realized that he was right and signed up immediately.

"Maybe I Should Work in Someone Else's Private Practice *First*"

It sounds counterintuitive, but I don't recommend working in someone else's private practice before starting your own.

Many people think that they should work in someone else's private practice before starting their own in order to gain experience. However, as much as I preach collaboration over competition, when employees of private practices leave to start their own practices, there are a range of outcomes— everything from well wishes to hurt feelings, awkwardness, and threats of legal action. Private practice owners don't really want to train people who are going to go out and compete with them. That's why many private practices have employees sign noncompete clauses. If you signed a noncompete clause and are planning to open your own practice, I recommend meeting with a lawyer to review the contract and understand your options.

Case Study
Meet Jessie Ginsburg, MS, CCC-SLP

Jessie started her private practice immediately after her clinical fellowship. She knew she wanted to start her own clinic, but her professors told her that she was too young and inexperienced. Rather than let that stop her, she dove in, gained experience, and is now internationally known for her work with autistic children. Jessie's practice, Pediatric Therapy Playhouse, is over 10 years old. Jessie has also launched an education business in which she teaches clinicians how to have more effective sessions with autistic clients. To learn more about Jessie, visit JessieGinsburg.com.

Jessie is an alum of The Grow Your Private Practice Program.

To hear Jessie's full story, listen to the Private Practice Success Stories podcast, Episode #74, "Growing Her Private Practice, Her Education Business, and Her Impact." Visit PrivatePracticeBook.com/Resources to listen to this episode and download our podcast playlist.

Case Study
Meet Claudia Davisson, MA, CCC-SLP

During her career, Claudia worked in various settings and never considered private practice. At age 53, she chose to start seeing clients on the side in order to supplement her retirement savings and joined The Start Your Private Practice Program™ to learn about private practice. She earned enough money to retire early and shift into private practice. Now, she's making significantly more than her school SLP salary by seeing clients herself and hiring contractors to see patients. Claudia's story is a wonderful reminder that you're not too old and it's not too late. As Claudia often says, "Old dogs can learn new tricks."

Claudia is an alum of The Start Your Private Practice Program™ and The Grow Your Private Practice Program and serves as a mentor in The Start Your Private Practice Program™.

To hear Claudia's full story, listen to the Private Practice Success Stories podcast, Episode #95, "You're Not Too Old and It's Not Too Late." Visit PrivatePracticeBook.com/Resources to listen to this episode and download our podcast playlist.

DON'T WAIT TO BECOME AN EXPERT TO START YOUR PRACTICE, OR YOU MAY NEVER START. INSTEAD, BECOME AN EXPERT AS YOU *build your practice.*

JENA H. CASTRO-CASBON, MS CCC-SLP

Takeaways

As long as you have something to bring to the table, you can start a private practice. Who decides whether you're good enough to start a private practice? You do. You are qualified to be in private practice if you choose to be.

How to Start a Private Practice without Breaking the *Bank*

My eyes darted around the large waiting room. As I looked around, I saw:

- Comfortable chairs and a large sofa for clients to sit on
- A busy receptionist answering phones and handing out clipboards
- Neatly organized toys
- Magazines on coffee tables
- Therapists coming in and taking waiting children back for their sessions
- A giant parking lot in the back

The space was gorgeous and had everything I could dream of in a clinic. It was such a cheerful and picture-perfect environment, a private practitioner's dream.

Behind the walls of the waiting room were more amazing spaces. Each clinician had their own office with a desk, a comfortable chair, and a computer. Bookcases and cabinets were full of therapy materials. In the hallway, there was a shelf with the most popular standardized assessments lined up one by one. Large closets were filled with all the therapy supplies and resources a clinician could ever dream of. At the end of the hallway there was a kitchen with a large table, a refrigerator, a water dispenser, a coffee maker, and more. Therapists buzzed up and down the hallway, smiling and greeting each other. Everyone looked friendly and happy. The therapists said they loved working there and loved the owner—and it was completely genuine. I couldn't wait until my private practice was like this, with all the bells and whistles. Someday.

But at the moment, I was 26 years old and didn't even have my first client yet. I dreamed of my future private practice all the time, especially over the weekends as the Sunday scaries set in.

My dreams turned into nightmares when I started totaling up all the expenses in my head. I knew I didn't have enough money to start the brick-and-mortar clinic I thought I needed. Between my low salary, school loans, and saving up for my wedding, cash was tight, and I knew it would continue to be tight if I didn't earn more money.

I started my private practice on a shoestring budget. I figured out the essential things I needed and used the money I earned to invest in my business and buy the bells and whistles over time.

The New Way to start a private practice is to start with the basics and use your earnings to invest in your business over time. If you don't know what you're doing, starting a private practice can cost you $5,000–$20,000 or more. If you know what you're doing, you can get started for around $400.

Average Start-Up Costs for Common Businesses

Business	Costs
Coffee shop[3]	$80,000 to $300,000 or more
Food truck[4]	$28,000 to $114,000 or more
Retail store[5]	$50,000 to $100,000 or more
Yoga studio[6]	$70,000 to $1,000,000 or more

Businesses that fail often take on too many expenses and/or don't have enough cash flow to turn a profit. In businesses with high start-up costs, you have to sell a lot of muffins, bracelets, or yoga classes to turn a profit in the first few years.

Most private practitioners charge $80–$150 per session. As a private practitioner, you can be profitable from the very beginning if you start with minimal overhead. I teach my students how to start their private practices debt-free (or as close to debt-free as possible). I don't want you to stack business loans on top of student loans. I can teach you how to be profitable from the very beginning.

If you're independently wealthy or have the money to buy everything you need for your clinic up front, then go for it. But be aware that spending money without money coming in can result in a lot of financial stress.

Case Study
Meet Danelle "Danni" Augustine, MS, CCC-SLP

Danni started a private practice in order to take control of her financial future. She opened a pediatric private practice in which she sees clients via private pay, insurance, and as a contractor for Early Steps (Louisiana's early intervention program). She started her practice debt-free (without a large initial investment) and was able to pay off $52,000 in debt and double her school SLP salary by focusing on keeping her expenses low. Danni is a huge advocate for clinicians increasing their financial literacy and learning how to become financially independent.

Danni is an alum of The Start Your Private Practice Program™.

To hear Danni's full story, listen to the Private Practice Success Stories podcast, Episode #168, "How to Increase Your Financial Security through Private Practice." Visit PrivatePracticeBook.com/Resources to listen to this episode and download our podcast playlist.

YOU CAN HAVE ALL THE
PRIVATE PRACTICE BELLS
AND WHISTLES ONE DAY,
but not on day one.

JENA H. CASTRO-CASBON, MS CCC-SLP

How to Start a Private Practice and Only Work with Ideal *Clients*

Who are your favorite clients—the ones that light you up and allow you to do your best work? What if you could work exclusively with the client populations that you're most confident in serving? In most traditional SLP and OT settings (schools, hospitals, early intervention programs, etc.), you work with anyone who's added to your caseload whether you feel competent to treat them or not.

In traditional settings, clinicians are pressured to be generalists and to treat anyone that's added to their caseload. Many clinicians have told me that they have tremendous anxiety and feelings of guilt working with clients that they don't feel comfortable or competent treating (and rightly so!).

One of my students told me that she signed up for as many CEU courses as she could so that she could be ready just in case she ever saw someone with a rarer issue. Although she felt knowledgeable, she didn't feel competent to treat some client populations because she didn't have enough deep knowledge. She was frustrated by how much time and money she spent collecting knowledge without using it; it left her feeling overwhelmed.

The SLP and OT fields are vast, and we can't know everything. What if you got to pick and choose the types of clients you work with? How cool would that be?

Working with Ideal *Clients*

When you have a private practice, you get to market your practice to attract your desired clinical population. If someone contacts you to inquire about a diagnosis or treatment approach that you aren't competent in, you can refer them to another provider instead of feeling unable to turn them away. If you focus on a small number of clinical populations, you'll likely start to specialize over time, but you don't have to.

Chances are you've heard people say that there aren't enough services for this or that population. Wouldn't it be wonderful if you could fill a void for services in your community? Private practice allows you to pursue your professional interests and focus or specialize in clinical populations that you love working with and who need your services.

What If I Want to Be a *Generalist*?

If you want to work with two different populations—like kids with feeding issues and adults with apraxia—it is possible. It's easier to become known for one thing than for two things—but it can be done. I recommend that if you want to reach two client groups, make two sets of marketing materials (brochures, etc.) that provide each population with relevant information, like treatment approaches and so forth.

Case Study
Meet Katja Piscitelli, MS, CCC-SLP

Katja is an SLP in Sacramento, California, who started her private practice soon after finishing graduate school. She started a neurodiversity-affirming private practice that offers speech and language therapy and augmentative and alternative communication (AAC) evaluations. She started her private practice when she still had a full-time job. Because she knew she wanted to leave her job quickly, Katja grew her private practice to a full-time level in just a few months. She has an active Instagram account (@BohoSpeechie) where she shares tips and strategies for working with Gestalt language processors.
Katja is an alum of The Start Your Private Practice Program™.

Case Study
Meet Tamiko "Tami" Teshima, MA, CCC-SLP

Tami started her private practice after being laid off from her school district job (before the Covid pandemic). She started a private practice to work with two unique populations: preschoolers needing speech and language therapy and teens and adults requiring gender-affirming voice and communication services. She lives in a small town in Michigan and wanted to bring these services to her community. During the Covid pandemic, she began to grow her private practice by hiring a mix of employees, contractors, and administrative support. Her practice now sees a wide variety of populations, and she has time to pursue other areas of interest, such as orofacial myofunctional therapy. Tami is a great example of someone who expanded her services according to her clinical interests.

Tami is an alum of The Start Your Private Practice Program™ and serves as a coach for The Grow Your Private Practice Program.

To hear Tami's full story, listen to the Private Practice Success Stories podcast, Episode #64, "Tots, Transgender Voice, and now . . . Telepractice." Visit PrivatePracticeBook.com/Resources to listen to this episode and download our podcast playlist.

WHEN YOU LOVE WORKING WITH YOUR IDEAL CLIENTS, YOU CAN FEEL IT, AND *they can feel it, too*.

JENA H. CASTRO-CASBON, MS CCC-SLP

Decision Time

What kinds of clients do you want to see in your private practice?

_____

_____

_____

_____

How to Start a Private Practice to Have More Balance in Your *Life*

"If you don't build your dream, someone else will hire you to help build theirs."
–Tony Gaskins

As I packed up my bag, I looked around the office. It was 7:30 p.m.

I had been at work since 7:30 a.m., as had most of the Speech Department. Although most of us were working 12-hour days, we were only paid for eight of those hours.

I had my "dream job" working at one of the most prestigious rehabilitation hospitals in the country. I felt incredibly lucky to get the job and have the name of that institution on my resume. When I wasn't at work, I was still working by planning sessions or taking continuing education courses. The hospital had an unspoken competition among colleagues about who was the best and/or most dedicated therapist.

In the beginning, I didn't mind working all the time. I was single and had a bunch of roommates who were SLPs and were working constantly too. For a while, it was fun to talk about work all the time, but eventually it got tiresome. Another year came and went without a raise. There was a bunch of turnover in the department because people weren't happy with the administrators. I became more and more frustrated with supervisors (especially non-SLPs) telling me how to do my job. I looked around and realized that the only people working there were new grads or lifers (people who had worked there for their entire careers). People stayed until they were in their late 20s or early 30s, then left when they needed more flexibility or suffered from early career burnout. The hospital hired an outside company to do an employee satisfaction study and then did nothing to improve morale. Management knew that it was easy to hire new grads who wanted to work there, so employee retention wasn't something they cared about very much.

Finally, I had had enough. I loved being an SLP and wanted to stay in love with the profession. Building my private practice was how I achieved that goal.

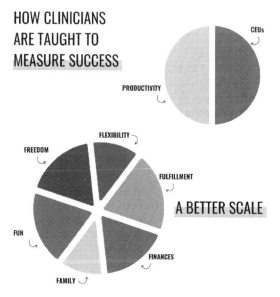

There's more to being successful than productivity and CEUs. Success is defined differently by each of us; here are a few components that I include in my definition:

- Having energy left for family time after work
- Leaving work at work

- Having the flexibility to be at important events
- Earning a salary that matches my education, experience, and skillset
- Having fun and feeling fulfilled in my work

I can do all this while making an impact on others' lives!

There is more to life than supporting the dreams of your employer.

One of the main reasons why SLPs and OTs pursue private practice is to have more work–life balance. One of the first things I have students in The Start Your Private Practice Program™ do is fill out a weekly schedule and determine when they can see clients.

For example, if you're in full control of your private practice hours, you can choose to:

- Not see clients before 10 a.m. in order to have a slower morning
- Stop seeing clients at 3 p.m. so you can pick up your kids from school
- Not see clients on Fridays so you can enjoy three-day weekends

You can (and should!) schedule your life first and then schedule your practice around your life. This gives you time for your priorities and time to rest and recharge, which staves off burnout.

Several clients in our programs have set up what they call "lifestyle private practices" in which they create their ideal schedule, figure out how much they want to earn, and then see only enough clients to reach their goals.

Case Study
Meet Sarah Sweeney, MEd, CCC-SLP

Sarah is an SLP in Mechanicsville, Virginia, who started her private practice after feeling trapped in a school job. In her private practice, she sees children for general speech and language services. She has a special interest in orofacial myofunctional disorders and pediatric feeding. One of the things that Sarah stresses is the importance of boundaries and how being firm with boundaries helps control burnout. Better work–life balance starts with creating (and sticking to!) boundaries.

Sarah is an alum of The Grow Your Private Practice Program.

To hear Sarah's full story, listen to the Private Practice Success Stories podcast, Episode #187, "From Getting Started to Starting to Grow." Visit PrivatePracticeBook.com/Resources to listen to this episode and download our podcast playlist.

YOU'VE INVESTED TOO MUCH IN YOUR CAREER TO LET YOURSELF GET *burned out by it.*

JENA H. CASTRO-CASBON, MS CCC-SLP

Conclusion

THE OLD WAY	THE NEW WAY
Brick & Mortar	Flexible Space
Wait 20+ Years to Start	Gain Experience As You Grow
High Start-Up Costs	Start Debt-Free and Profitable
Scarcity Mindset	Abundance Mindset
Start Full-Time	Start Part-Time
No Diversity	Diversity
Big Practice	Any Size Practice

the INDEPENDENT CLINICIAN

There are a lot of myths and misconceptions about private practice that keep clinicians from pursuing it. When most people think about private practice, they're thinking about the Old Way. It's much easier to build a practice using the New Way, which make it easier, faster, and cheaper to get started. My mission is to make the process of starting and growing private practices easier for SLPs and OTs. That way, you can focus on doing what you do best: helping people.

So far, we've covered why SLPs and OTs go into private practice and how starting your practice using the New Way can save you a lot of time, money, and frustration and allow you to create the life you've imagined. I hope you're excited about the possibilities that come with private practice and that you're eager to learn how to get started.

Chapter 3:
The Private Practice Success Path

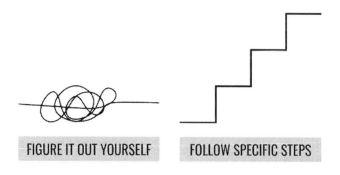

FIGURE IT OUT YOURSELF   FOLLOW SPECIFIC STEPS

When you're first starting out, it can be really overwhelming to think about how you're going to build a private practice, especially without a business background. Before you start a private practice, you need to know what steps to take and in what order you need to take them. You ascend a staircase one step at a time; starting a private practice is the same. But there are lots of people who guess their way through the process—that's how they end up feeling overwhelmed.

For those who like to follow tried and true steps, I've created the five-step Private Practice Success Path to lead you into private practice with all your ducks in a row. It's important to go through each of these phases in order, because they build on each other.

Disclaimer: There are a lot of steps to start a private practice, many more than I can cover in this book. At this end of this chapter, I'll share how you can get a full list of all of the steps.

Step 1: Picture Your Private *Practice*

You wouldn't build a house without architectural plans, right? In the same way, you need a plan for your private practice. You need to have a vision of your ideal private practice.

To help you with this, I have included a Private Practice Plan worksheet in the Book Bonuses. This resource will help you make your first five decisions as a private practitioner. To access it, please visit PrivatePracticeBook.com/Resources.

Decision 1: Why Do You Want a Private *Practice?*

Let's start with your why.

Why do you want a private practice? When you start a private practice, you need to know your reasons for doing so. Knowing your why, your driving force, will keep you focused when things are tough.

Knowing your why will push you forward and keep you from giving up.

Most clinicians start private practices because there are things they want more (or less) of in their lives.

The Car *Analogy*

I don't think of private practice as a job setting; I think of it as a vehicle to get you where you want to go. When you're in the driver's seat of the private practice vehicle, you choose what to drive toward and what to drive away from.

What Do You Want to Drive *Toward?*

When I ask clinicians to share why they want to be in private practice, they usually say things like:

- "I want to create a better life for myself and my family."
- "I want more work–life balance."
- "I want to provide high-quality care without worrying about productivity and numbers."
- "I want to feel like I'm truly helping clients in the most individualized way possible."

These all also go back to my favorite F words in Chapter 1. Basically, clinicians want more freedom, flexibility, fulfillment, finances, and time for family and fun.

When you're driving your own private practice vehicle, you can drive toward a more flexible schedule, a higher salary, working only with ideal clients, and more.

Start thinking about what you want to drive toward.

What Do You Want to Drive Away *From?*

Now that you've decided what you want more of, it's time to look in the rearview mirror and think about what you want to drive away from.

Maybe you want to drive away from high caseloads, micromanaging bosses and supervisors, unrealistic expectations, endless paperwork, and required attendance at meetings that don't matter.

Think about what you want to drive away from.

Who Is in the Car With *You?*

As you drive toward what you want and away from what you don't want, you also have an opportunity to pick who is in the car with you.

You can be in the car by yourself as a solo practitioner. You can also add employees or contractors to help support you and your business.

Which Path Will You Take? And How Quickly Will You *Go?*

You'll also choose the path you take in your car. Perhaps you'll go toward individual therapy, or maybe you'll take a route that includes group therapy and IEP consultations. You can also determine how quickly or slowly to drive your private practice vehicle. You may want to get your practice up and running quickly, or you may choose to move more slowly, keeping your business small until you're ready to grow it.

Are You Stuck on a *Bus?*

I've shared the car analogy many times in our private practice workshops. People often say that they feel like they're stuck on a bus that their employer is driving. One person even said she felt like she was locked in the trunk! When someone else is driving, you don't have control of where you're going or who's with you. Maybe you don't like the direction your employer is going, or maybe your company is understaffed. The only way to get off the bus is to quit your job.

Take the wheel and start driving your own private practice vehicle. When you're the driver, you're in full control of where you're going and how you get there.

PRIVATE PRACTICE IS A VEHICLE TO GET YOU
where you want to go.

JENA H. CASTRO-CASBON, MS CCC-SLP

Decision Time What is your why?

_____

_____

_____

_____

Reflect on the car analogy as you fill out the chart **below.**

Drive toward	Drive away from	Who's in the car with you?

Knowing your why, your driving force, for starting and growing a private practice will keep you focused on your future. Most private practitioners have a very clear why; knowing your why is most important when challenges arise and you need a push to keep going.

Case Study
Meet Kristin Kudarauskas, MS, CCC-SLP

Kristin is a private practitioner who serves children and adults in Fredericksburg, Virginia. Being of service to the community is one of Kristin's values, so she founded Chancellor Therapy Solutions to provide effective, evidence-based speech therapy for the whole family. Kristin's desire to start and grow her private practice in order to serve her local community was deeply rooted in her faith.

Kristin is an alum of The Start Your Private Practice Program™ and The Grow Your Private Practice Program.

To hear Kristin's full story, listen to the Private Practice Success Stories podcast, Episode #184, "Faith and Private Practice." Visit PrivatePractice-Book.com/Resources to listen to this episode and download our podcast playlist.

Decision 2: Who Will You Help?

In private practice, you have an opportunity to choose which clients you'll work with. In school and hospital settings, you don't usually have any say in who's added to your caseload. This can be overwhelming, because you may feel like you're being asked to treat patients that you don't feel competent enough to do a good job with. In private practice, you not only can choose clients that you love working with—you can also choose the treatment approaches that you feel most comfortable using. If you love working with a specific population, limit your practice to that population.

Identify populations that align with your clinical experience and interests and the needs in your local community.

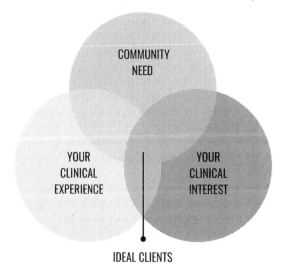

COMMUNITY NEED

YOUR CLINICAL EXPERIENCE

YOUR CLINICAL INTEREST

IDEAL CLIENTS

You can also consider whether you want to be a specialist or a generalist. Generalists work with a wide variety of ages and diagnoses; specialists work with niche populations. To get your private practice off the ground, I recommend starting off as a generalist and working with any client population that you feel comfortable and competent treating.

Specialists and niche-focused clinicians tend to become known as the go-to experts for a particular diagnosis or disorder, which is great for word-of-mouth marketing. Becoming an expert and/or having a niche allows you to be a big fish in a small pond.

Case Study
Meet Asha LeRay, MS, OTR/L

Asha is an occupational therapist in Boston, Massachusetts, who started her private practice, Inclusive OT, after suffering from burnout in the school system. Her expertise lies in treating children with physical and medical complexities, feeding disorders, and food allergies. She found her first two clients within a month of opening her practice. Asha resigned from her full-time job and took a part-time job so that she could focus on building her private practice. She says that her private practice has led to "the rejuvenation of my burned out career, increased income, and a new skill set."

Asha is an alum of The Start Your Private Practice Program™ and a student in The Grow Your Private Practice Program.

IN PRIVATE PRACTICE, YOU HAVE THE OPPORTUNITY TO WORK WITH CLIENTS *who light you up* AND ALLOW YOU TO DO YOUR BEST WORK.

JENA H. CASTRO-CASBON, MS CCC-SLP

Decision Time

Who do you want to treat?

_____

_____

_____

_____

_____

_____

_____

Decision 3: What Services Will You Offer?

In private practice, you get to choose what services you'll offer. Private practitioners aren't limited to offering individual therapy and evaluations; many offer additional services.

Here's a list of services that SLPs and OTs offer through their private practices:

- Individual therapy
- Group therapy
- Evaluations
- Telepractice
- Consultations
- Workshops
- Intensives
- Special services
- Animal-assisted interventions
- IEP consultations
- Camps
- Advocacy
- Parent coaching
- Parent classes
- Paid products
- Expert witness services
- Public speaking

This is not an exhaustive list—you're only limited by your creativity!

What types of services you offer is your decision. If you love doing groups, fantastic. But if you're burned out on doing groups and never want to do one again, you don't have to.

Just as most private practitioners don't start off with a brick-and-mortar clinic, they also don't start out offering a million services. Start with a few things and grow from there. You have a unique opportunity to choose services that your clients need and you love to deliver, so I encourage you to think outside the box!

Case Study
Meet Gloriner "Glory" Lichon, MA, CCC-SLP

Glory is an Air Force veteran, SLP, and founder of Glow Bright Therapy. Glory was a school-based SLP who left the school setting due to burnout. She started a telepractice with a mission to provide accessible services to children in rural areas and underserved early intervention counties. Her telepractice company employs SLPs from across the country, serves clients in eight states, and is still growing!

Glory is an alum of The Grow Your Private Practice Program.

To hear Glory's full story, listen to the Private Practice Success Stories podcast Episode #137, "Building a Telepractice Company." Visit PrivatePracticeBook.com/Resources to listen to this episode and download our podcast playlist.

LOVE GROUPS? GREAT — OFFER THEM THROUGH YOUR PRIVATE PRACTICE! NEVER WANT TO DO A GROUP AGAIN?
You don't have to!

JENA H. CASTRO-CASBON, MS CCC-SLP

Decision Time

What services do you want to offer clients?

_____

_____

_____

_____

Decision 4: Where Will You Treat Clients?

Choosing where you'll see private clients is a big decision. You don't need to have an expensive brick- and-mortar space in order to see private clients. There are many other options to consider before starting a brick-and-mortar clinic.

Here's what I call the CCCs of location:

- Cheap and affordable when you're starting out
- Convenient for you and your clients
- Comfortable for you and your clients (e.g., some people don't like home visits)

If you plan to offer in-person services, it's easiest to start out as a mobile therapist and see clients in their homes, schools, daycare facilities, workplaces, or a community location. Seeing clients in their own space not only results in better therapy—it's also convenient for the clients and usually results in better client carryover. It's also a very quick and inexpensive way to get started in private practice.

Case Study
Meet Michelle C. Eliason, MS, OTR/L, CKTS, CBIS

Michelle is an adult-focused private OT practice owner in Buffalo, New York. She started her private practice debt-free from her kitchen table and traveled to clients homes. Since then, she has grown her business to include two neurological and physical restorative outpatient practices. She also runs an online mentorship and resource site for OT students and practitioners. Michelle is proof that you can start a private practice on a shoestring budget and invest in your business in order to grow it.

Michelle is a mentor for The Start Your Private Practice Program™.

To hear Michelle's full story, listen to the Private Practice Success Stories podcast Episode #183, "From Her Kitchen Table to Two Locations." Visit PrivatePracticeBook.com/Resources to listen to this episode and download our podcast playlist.

Before the Covid pandemic, very few private practitioners offered teletherapy. During the pandemic, nearly 100% of therapists switched to teletherapy.[1,2] Online services are convenient for both clinician and client because neither party has to travel. Start-up expenses include a computer and software, but these are very affordable. Today, more and more private practitioners are offering telepractice either exclusively or as one of their service delivery options.

Another option is to see clients in your home. This option is particularly advantageous if you have extra space and want to save time by having your clients come to you. However, you need to check your homeowners insurance policy and research any zoning restrictions to ensure you can conduct business in your home. Requirements may include a separate business entrance and wheelchair accessibility, so you may have to modify your home. Another common requirement is to provide a private location within your home. Given these requirements, this option may not work for everyone.

Case Study
Meet Emily McCullough, MA, CCC-SLP

Emily is a private practitioner based in Austin, Texas, who sees pediatric clients via telepractice from the comfort of her home. She started her telepractice during the Covid pandemic and grew it to a full-time level. Emily founded Parade Pediatric Speech Therapy to provide a safe space for all kids and families on their communication journey.

Emily is an alum The Start Your Private Practice Program™.

To hear Emily's full story, listen to the Private Practice Success Stories podcast Episode #110, "Building a Private Practice and Safe Space for LGBTQ+ Clients and Families." Visit PrivatePracticeBook.com/Resources to listen to this episode and download our podcast playlist.

Last, you can have a brick-and-mortar practice. Depending on where you live and how large the location is, it can cost anywhere from a couple hundred dollars to several thousand dollars a month for a space. There are other considerations for a brick-and-mortar office as well. You have to furnish it with things like desks, chairs, bookcases, and everything else that goes into an office space. Additional costs include extra insurance, utilities, internet connection, cleaning fees, and so on. For this reason, most private practitioners don't start with a brick-and-mortar office.

Case Study
Meet Lisa Geary, MS, CCC-SLP

Lisa is a private practitioner in Yorktown, Virginia. She started her practice after 25 years of experience working in schools, consulting with an AAC company, and working as a clinical assistant professor. Lisa decided to start her private practice by utilizing space inside her husband's dental practice. Lisa is proof that there are many creative solutions for where you can see clients!

Lisa is an alum of The Start Your Private Practice Program™ and The Grow Your Private Practice Program.

To hear Lisa's full story, listen to the Private Practice Success Stories podcast, Episode #185, "Starting and Growing Her Private Practice in One Year." Visit PrivatePracticeBook.com/Resources to listen to this episode and download our podcast playlist.

YOU CAN START YOUR PRIVATE PRACTICE OUT OF YOUR KITCHEN, YOUR TRUNK, YOUR HOUSE OR A CLINIC.
Just start.

JENA H. CASTRO-CASBON, MS CCC-SLP

Decision Time
Where do you want to see your private clients?

_____

_____

Decision 5: When Will You See Your Clients?

Deciding when to see private clients usually starts by looking at your calendar. I teach people to start seeing private clients on the side while keeping a full-time job with its steady pay and benefits (this also gives you a chance to test the private practice waters). Most of the students in The Start Your Private Practice Program™ start by seeing private clients after work, on the weekends, on days off, or during the summer before transitioning to full-time private practice.

I encourage you to do the math and figure out how many clients you can see during a typical week. Start with one session. Then try three or four sessions a week. You have a private practice even if you have just a handful of clients. Actually, having just a handful of clients can be pretty lucrative.

That's exactly what I did.

I saw clients after work and on the weekends. I had a 9–5 job that changed to 10-hour shifts, four days a week. So, I saw clients on Fridays and Sundays. Working four 10 hour days and seeing clients on the weekend was a great way to start, but it was also exhausting. So I switched to 32 hours a week: two 10-hour days and three half days. That way, I was able to see private clients on the half days.

You may feel like you don't have time to see clients, but if you want the freedom, flexibility, fulfillment, and financial independence that come with private practice, I'm sure you can find at least an hour each week. Then, you can gradually reduce your hours at your current job (if possible) in order to see more clients.

Keep your eyes on the prize. In other words, envision your private practice from the very beginning. Eventually, you'll be earning enough money to leave your job and go all in on your private practice, which is Stage 3: Grow Your Private Practice.

Case Study
Meet Dr. Dani Gaff (Newcombe) SLPD, CCC-SLP

Dani is a school-based SLP who lives in Indiana. She wanted to further her reach in her community, beyond the students she was seeing in her school. Her private practice not only allowed her to see more children, but she also found she was able to include children who need/communicate using augmentative and alternative communication. She says that seeing ideal clients through her own practice helped decrease her feelings of burnout.

Dani is an alum of The Start Your Private Practice Program™. You can follow her on Instagram: @TheMessySLP.

To hear Dani's full story, listen to the Private Practice Success Stories podcast, Episode #148, "Working with Ideal Clients Outside of My School SLP Job." Visit PrivatePracticeBook.com/Resources to listen to this episode and download our podcast playlist.

Decision Time
When will you see your clients?

_____

_____

_____

_____

_____

Mon	Tues	Wed	Thurs	Fri	Sat	Sun

Check out the Private Practice Schedule Maker in the Book Bonuses. This resource will help you identify when you can see private clients. To access it, please visit PrivatePracticeBook.com/Resources.

Takeaways

You can design a private practice and a life that you absolutely love.

Take the time to carefully plan who, what, when, and where before you start your practice so that you know what you're building.

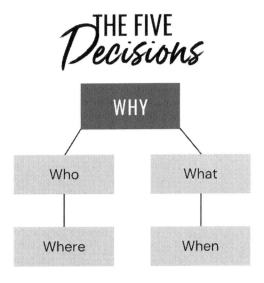

This section presented many considerations regarding how to picture your perfect private practice. Now, you can dream and make decisions. In the next section, we'll discuss how to protect yourself and your private practice.

Don't forget to take the decisions you've made and add them to your Private Practice Plan worksheet, available in the Book Bonuses. To access it, please visit: PrivatePracticeBook.com/Resources.

THERE'S NO SUCH THING AS A PERFECT PRIVATE PRACTICE—THERE'S ONLY THE PRIVATE PRACTICE *that's perfect for you.*

JENA H. CASTRO-CASBON, MS CCC-SLP

Step 2: Protect Your Private Practice

"Risk comes from not knowing what you're doing."
—Warren Buffet

Protecting your private practice is the second phase of the Private Practice Success Path. This is where you get your ducks in a row and build your practice on a strong foundation.

It's better to be safe than sorry, right? After you invest in learning how to start a private practice, you should invest in protecting your private practice. If you want to work on your own, under your own license, it's important to make sure you're protected before you start seeing clients. Even if you're just seeing one or two clients on the side, legally speaking, you still have a private practice and you need protection. We live in a litigious society. Although lawsuits in private practice are fairly rare, they can happen.[3]

Note that I am an SLP, not a lawyer—so don't take anything you read here as official legal advice. If you have legal questions, please meet with a lawyer in your area who is familiar with local laws.

Reduce Professional Risk

First, reduce professional risk by getting professional liability insurance; this protects your license. Obviously, you must also follow the code of ethics and local, state, and federal laws. If you lose your license, you can't practice, so don't risk this.

Make sure to document your services. A lot of people think that in private practice—especially if you're private pay—you don't have to do documentation. That's a myth. I would love to tell you that you don't have to document your services, but it's not true. The good news is that you get to choose how to document your services.

Reduce Financial Risk

To reduce financial risk, start by seeing clients on the side. That way, you'll have steady pay and benefits as you begin seeing private clients and building your practice. You'll have money coming in until your private practice brings in enough income on its own. Not taking on a lot of overhead at the beginning is another way to minimize financial risk.

Reduce Legal Risk

Two ways to decrease the legal risks associated with private practice are to have a formal business designation (such as an LLC) and to have clients sign legal forms acknowledging that they've been informed of and understand your policies (e.g., attendance policy, fee schedule, HIPAA forms, etc.). Rules vary from state to state. The full list of steps to decrease your risks is covered in The Start Your Private Practice Program™.

Check the Book Bonuses for a free, downloadable HIPAA policy you can use in your private practice. The policy is part of the Private Practice Clinic Forms pack, a set of 30+ lawyer-reviewed forms for private practitioners. Visit PrivatePracticeBook.com/Resources to grab it.

What if I Make a Mistake?

Many SLPs and OTs are so worried about making mistakes that they never start. Countless people have asked me, "But what if I end up in SLP/OT jail?" First, don't do anything illegal. Second, you'll probably make a few mistakes, but you'll learn from them. For example, if you make a billing error, just resubmit the claim.

Get your ducks in a row as you build your practice.

JENA H. CASTRO-CASBON, MS CCC-SLP

Takeaways

A private practice is a legitimate business, and you need to think of yours as such. It's better to be safe than to be sorry. Protection doesn't cost as much as you think, and minimizing risk is very important, especially as you begin. Once you have legal protection in place, you can take care of the following steps.

Step 3: Promote Your Private Practice

"Marketing is really just about sharing your passion."
—Michael Hyatt

Now that you have your legal affairs in order, it's time to market your private practice.

Many SLPs and OTs worry about marketing because they don't have a marketing background and are scared of being perceived as pushy. In reality, marketing is simply communicating about the services you offer to people who need those services or to people who know people who need those services, such as allied health professionals, pediatricians, support group leaders, and so forth.

Explain the services you offer in a way that communicates who you are and how you help people. If you lead with how you help people, you won't be perceived as pushy. Being pushy is when you think everyone needs your services. If you're not trying to treat people who don't need treatment, you're not being pushy. Very few clinicians are overly pushy; quite the opposite—many students in our programs need to learn how to be more assertive in communicating about their practices.

Why is it so important to market your practice? Because if people don't know about you, they can't hire you. If you want to see clients, you need to market your services using whatever marketing strategy feels right to you. The bottom line is that you must tell people about your practice in order to get clients.

The Need for SLP and OT Services

There is a huge need for SLP and OT services. In most areas, there are long wait lists for services at clinics and hospitals—that means that there are not enough providers in the area.

Rural Areas

If you live in a more rural area and you're concerned that there aren't enough clients to be seen, I'm here to tell you that that isn't true. Plenty of people are going without services in rural communities.[4,5] Some patients drive for hours to reach the closest available provider. You can be a solution to that need.

Case Study
Meet Martha Horrocks, MEd, CCC-SLP

Martha is an SLP in private practice who sees primarily fluency clients via telepractice across the state of Maine. She also offers consulting services and sells therapy materials and other digital materials online. She is a proud Mainer and loves being able to see clients in all parts of her state without leaving the comfort of her home. Balance is very important to Martha. She created multiple streams of income in order to help support her family financially while maintaining a balanced life.

Martha is an alum of The Start Your Private Practice Program™.

To hear Martha's full story, listen to the Private Practice Success Stories podcast, Episode #139, "Balancing Her Life, Telepractice-Based Practice, and TpT Business." Visit PrivatePracticeBook.com/Resources to listen to this episode and download our podcast playlist.

Populated Areas

In cities, there are more private practices, but there are also more people, and there are still plenty of people going without services or stuck on wait lists. So, if you live in a big city, don't be discouraged and think, "There are already so many private practices!" Yes, there are many private practices, but there are also many people who still need services.

Case Study
Meet Meera Raval (Deters), CCC-SLP, BCTS

Meera is an SLP with her own private practice in Houston, Texas. She has a mobile concierge practice that serves children from 18 months through 12 years old. Meera specializes in working with children who have speech, language, and social/pragmatic issues. She is a Board Certified Teleprac-tice Specialist. Meera works four days a week and has built her schedule to include time for lunch with her parents twice a week.

Meera is an alum of The Start Your Private Practice Program™.

To hear Meera's full story, listen to the Private Practice Success Sto-ries podcast, Episode #150, "Owning a Private Practice in a Big City." Visit PrivatePracticeBook.com/Resources to listen to this episode and download our podcast playlist.

Marketing

Private Client Opportunities Can Pop Up Randomly

Sometimes opportunities to see private clients fall into people's laps.

That's what happened to me. When my first opportunity came up, I still thought I wouldn't be seeing private clients for a couple of decades. The first few times I was asked if I saw private clients, I said, "No." But eventually I said, "Yes!" and started with my first private client.

Here's my all-time favorite story of how The Start Your Private Practice Program™ alum got her first client. One day, Christina Bennett, MS, CCC-SLP, was wearing a cute SLP pride T-shirt and decided to go to Subway for lunch. While she was in line, a woman came up to her and said, "Oh, my goodness, are you a speech pathologist?"

Christina said, "Yes, I am."

"Well, I have a son who's autistic and nonverbal, and he needs services. We haven't been able to find them. Are you able to see him?"

She smiled and said, "Sure! I can see him in my private practice."

That was how she got her first client. It's a wonderful example of how random opportunities can arise. That's why it's important to have all of your ducks in a row—so you'll be ready when opportunity strikes!

Relationship Marketing

Another great way to get your first clients is through relationship marketing.

Relationship-based referrals happen when you tell friends, family, and professional connections that you're seeing private clients. Because they know you, the quality of your work, and the types of clients that you'd like to see, these tend to be great referrals.

If you're worried about being pushy, when someone asks what you've been up to, just say:

"I started a private practice. If you know any families who are looking for services for [children, adults, or both] with [the following diagnosis, disorder, or difference] who want help to develop [the following skills], please let them know that I just opened a private practice and I don't have a wait list yet."

That's all you have to say. Relationship marketing is important because it leads to word-of-mouth referrals. You can't get word-of-mouth referrals unless people know about you and you give them something to talk about.

Website

Having a website is essential, because people go online when they're looking for services. When someone searches for "speech therapy in St. Louis," they're actively looking to hire. You don't need a complicated or expensive website. Think of a website as a digital brochure, posted on the internet. The average annual cost of entry-level web hosting is a little over $100 per year.[6] Until you can afford a really nice website, you can simply use the templates that most web hosting companies offer for free with paid hosting services.

Social Media

Some people can't wait to market themselves via social media; others want nothing to do with social media marketing.

Social media marketing can be very effective, but it can also be a waste of time. In order to get the maximum benefit from social media marketing, you have to consistently create content, which is more time-consuming than most people realize. Even if you do post all the time, you don't have control over who sees your posts; that's dictated by the algorithms for whatever platform you're on. Unfortunately, the algorithms prioritize paid ads over free content.

I know several people who got their first clients through social media; however, many of them already had social media skills and followers to tap into.

Social media works, but it's a slower strategy. Some beginners use social media because it makes them feel like they're actively marketing—but they may be avoiding more intimate and effective marketing methods, like relationship marketing.

IF PEOPLE DON'T KNOW ABOUT YOU, *they cant hire you.*

JENA H. CASTRO-CASBON, MS CCC-SLP

Put yourself out there and make sure that people know about you and your services.

In The Start Your Private Practice Program™, we teach students how to get their first clients in the quickest and most efficient ways possible. In fact, most students get their first client within a few weeks of marketing their new business, proving that you can get your first client very quickly if you know what you're doing. We focus on free and inexpensive strategies in order to keep start-up costs as low as possible and help people pay off their investment quickly. As your private practice grows, you'll most likely establish a dedicated marketing budget.

Decision Time

What marketing strategies are you excited to use to get your first clients?

_____

_____

_____

_____

Takeaways

You don't have to have a marketing background or be sales-y in order to get clients, but you do have to put yourself out there and tell people you're starting a practice. There are free or cheap ways to get your first clients, so you don't have to spend a ton of money on advertising—but you need to know what to do.

Activity

Want to get more comfortable talking about your (future) private practice? Get into the habit of telling people that you have a private practice. You can even say "small private practice," if that makes you more comfortable.

Make a plan to tell five *strangers* that you have a private practice. They can be random people, parents at an event for your kid, or new acquaintances. Then, do the same thing with five people that you know.

The goal is to practice saying, "I have a private practice." Develop a habit of saying it whenever the opportunity arises. Even if you don't have clients yet, you can start telling people that you have a small private practice. One student in The Start Your Private Practice Program™ told me that she told strangers on a ski lift about her private practice while they were riding up the mountain!

Marketing gets easier with time—but only if you practice.

Step 4: Get Paid in Private Practice

"You can have everything in life you want, if you will just help
other people get what they want."
—Zig Ziglar

When you're setting up a private practice, you need to pick what payer sources to accept.

Money may not be your primary driver, but your business needs money to survive. If your business doesn't bring in enough money, you'll have to shut down. If you shut down, you won't be able to help people. So, let's make sure you're bringing in enough money to be profitable from the beginning.

As part of the planning process, start by setting financial goals. Maybe you only want to earn a couple hundred extra dollars a month; maybe you want to double or triple your current salary. Once you've identified your goal, calculate how many sessions you'll need in order to reach it.

For example, if you want to earn an extra $400 per month, you only need to see one client per week if you charge $100 per session:

$100 per hour × 1 session per week × 4 weeks = $400 per month

This same equation can also help you calculate what you need to do to save up for big-ticket items such as a wedding, a down payment on a house, a family vacation, or a kitchen renovation. You can adjust any of the variables: see more clients, charge a higher rate, or increase both. In either case, you have to know your goal in order to be able to create a plan.

If you want a raise, give yourself the raise by treating private clients instead of waiting for your employer to take action. If you want to leave your job, calculate how many clients you need in order to replace your salary.

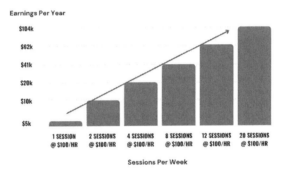

Work smarter, not harder

BY SEEING PRIVATE CLIENTS

How many sessions can you do?

Earnings Per Year

| | 1 SESSION @ $100/HR | 2 SESSIONS @ $100/HR | 4 SESSIONS @ $100/HR | 8 SESSIONS @ $100/HR | 12 SESSIONS @ $100/HR | 20 SESSIONS @ $100/HR |

Sessions Per Week

(Note: This is pre-tax income.)

In private practice, there is no ceiling on your income. In schools and hospitals, you're capped at a certain salary. It takes years or decades to move up the career ladder. In private practice, if you want to earn more money, you simply take on more clients. The next section presents an overview of different methods of receiving payment. In The Start Your Private Practice Program™, we teach you how to get set up for each of these methods.

IN PRIVATE PRACTICE, THERE *is no ceiling on your income*.

JENA H. CASTRO-CASBON, MS CCC-SLP

Private Pay

Many private practices start as private pay only. Some practitioners stay with private pay only because they don't want to deal with insurance or have limitations on what services they can provide.

If you only take private pay, choose how much to charge for your services. I cringe whenever someone asks me, "What's the going rate for therapy services in [location]?" I don't like that question, because it doesn't account for the skill of the provider. For example, if two providers—a new clinician and a clinical expert—are both charging $125 per session, the "going rate" doesn't necessarily reflect the value of their services.

One reason why I recommend that you start out as a private-pay-only practice is that it's easy to get set up. You can start with private pay clients as soon as you have a rate and a method to collect payment. You can stay with private pay long-term, or you can see a mix of private pay and insurance clients.

If you're not sure what to charge, it's better to pick a private pay rate that feels good to you and increase it as the value of your clinical skills increases.

Case Study
Meet Kristin Beasley, MA, CCC-SLP

Kristin has a private-pay-only practice in Glendale, Arizona. She joined The Start Your Private Practice Program™ and got three clients within two weeks. By the end of her first month, she had ten private pay clients. She started her practice by seeing private clients on the side, keeping her school SLP job. She also had three young children. Kristin says she told her family that as she built her private practice, she would be passing through a busy season in order to have more time and freedom later. A few years later, she has a thriving private pay clinic and more balance for her family.

Kristin is an alum of The Start Your Private Practice Program™ and The Grow Your Private Practice Program.

To hear Kristin's full story, listen to the Private Practice Success Stories podcast, Episode #164, "Creating Balance and Joy Through Her Full-Time Private Practice." Visit PrivatePracticeBook.com/Resources to listen to this episode and download our podcast playlist.

Insurance

Many private practitioners become providers for commercial insurance plans. In order to be considered an in-network provider by insurance companies, you have to complete an application. Then, you submit claims. The insurance company processes the claims and pays you their contracted rate. Because many families prefer to go through insurance to get therapy, you can find a lot of clients this way.

Before providing therapy, make sure that the treatment approach you intend to use is covered; this will ensure that you get paid. Contracted rates and the time frame for payment vary among health insurance companies.

Medicare

Medicare is a federal health insurance program for people over 65 and certain younger people with qualifying disabilities. If you're a private practitioner who wants to work with Medicare-eligible adults, you have to become a Medicare provider and bill through Medicare. Before providing therapy, make sure that the services you plan to offer are covered by Medicare. Medicare tends to pay fairly well and on time.

At the time of this writing, SLPs and OTs are not allowed to bill private pay for Medicare-eligible adults.[7] It is my sincere hope that this rule will be changed in the future. Please consult ASHA or AOTA (American Occupational Therapy Association) for guidance.

Case Study
Meet Katie Brown, MA, CCC-SLP, CBIS

Katie is an adult-focused private practitioner in Buffalo, New York, whose primary form of payment is Medicare. Katie says she started her private practice for two reasons: to provide evidence-based, holistic, and person-centered care for adults with acquired brain injuries and to spend more time with her family. Katie's private practice is booming, despite the presence of a large hospital in town. She's set herself apart from the other clinic and keeps hiring additional clinicians to keep up with demand and to avoid having a wait list. Katie's adult-focused practice is thriving and proves that private practice isn't just for pediatric clinicians. Katie is an alum of The Start Your Private Practice Program and now serves as a mentor.

To hear Katie's full story, listen to the Private Practice Success Stories podcast, Episode #121, "Adult- Focused Private Practice Success." Visit PrivatePracticeBook.com/Resources to listen to this episode and download our podcast playlist.

Medicaid

Medicaid is a public insurance program that provides healthcare coverage to low-income families and people with disabilities. Because Medicaid is regulated at the state level, you'll need to contact your state Medicaid office for an application and to learn what's required. Reimbursement varies by state, and private practitioners report that the rates are often lower than those offered by commercial insurance.

Financially, the difference between private pay and third-party payers comes down to volume. With private pay, you can earn more while seeing a lower volume of clients. With third-party payers, your per-session reimbursement will (likely) be less, so you'll have to see a higher volume of clients to earn the same amount of money. It all comes down to what you want to do!

Case Study
Meet Adrienne Fuller, MS, CCC-SLP

Adrienne is the owner and clinical director of Speech Builders, LLC, outside Orlando, Florida. Her multidisciplinary practice employs clinical and nonclinical staff and serves hundreds of families a month. She accepts a variety of commercial insurance plans as well as Medicaid. Adrienne has expanded her impact and income by writing a book, *Get Your Toddler Talking*.

Adrienne is a coach for The Grow Your Private Practice Program.

To hear Adrienne's full story, listen to the Private Practice Success Stories podcast, Episode #103, "The Confidence You Need to Follow Your Dreams." Visit PrivatePracticeBook.com/Resources to listen to this episode and download our podcast playlist.

A Creative Payment Option: Scholarship Programs

Some clients receive scholarships and grants to pay for therapy services. Private practitioners are usually paid privately out of these funds. Scholarship programs present a wonderful opportunity for clients to get private therapy services and are yet another option for practitioners in terms of payer sources.

Case Study
Meet Amanda Modrowski, MA, CCC-SLP

Amanda is a private practitioner in Toledo, Ohio, who has built her private practice with savvy (and helpful!) marketing strategies, such as preschool screenings. She recently began networking and participating in a study group with local dentists, orthodontists, oral surgeons, and ENTs in order to build the orofacial myofunctional therapy side of her practice. Amanda is a provider for the Jon Peterson Special Needs (JPSN) scholarship program, which provides scholarships for eligible children to receive therapy. At the time of this writing, about 70% of her revenue comes from seeing children who are recipients of this scholarship.

Amanda is an alum of The Start Your Private Practice Program™ and Grow Your Private Practice Ptaxrograms and currently serves as a mentor for The Start Your Private Practice Program™.

To hear Amanda's full story, listen to the Private Practice Success Stories podcast, Episode #138, "How to Put Yourself Out There." Visit PrivatePracticeBook.com/Resources to listen to this episode and download our podcast playlist.

YOU HAVE A MASTER'S DEGREE — IT'S TIME TO
earn like it!

JENA H. CASTRO-CASBON, MS CCC-SLP

Takeaways

I highly recommend determining your financial goals and doing the math to understand how many sessions you need at your chosen rate in order to reach your goals. There are several ways to get paid in private practice, from private pay to insurance to Medicare and Medicaid. Some private practitioners feel strongly about which payer sources they want to accept, knowing that there are pros and cons for each source. You can choose to accept one method or a combination of methods. There's no such thing as a "going rate," so set your rate based on the value of your services and increase it as you add more value.

Decision Time

What payer source(s) are you going to accept?

- ☐ Private Pay
- ☐ Insurance
- ☐ Medicare
- ☐ Medicaid
- ☐ Scholarship Programs
- ☐ Other: ___

Set a Financial Goal

I want to earn $_____ per month through my private practice.

In order to do that, I need to see ____ clients per week and charge $ ____ per session.

I created a handy calculator for you to play with the numbers. Look for the Private Practice Salary Calculator in the Book Bonuses at PrivatePracticeBook. com/Resources.

Step 5: Prepare to Grow Your Private Practice

"Be the CEO your parents wanted you to marry."
—unknown

The Shift toward Full-Time Private Practice

The last phase in the Private Practice Success Path is the prepare to grow phase. I firmly believe that starting on the side is the best way to start your private practice. However, it's not the best way to grow. If you're working for someone else, you can only operate your private practice for so many hours a day. Growing your private practice allows you to increase your impact and your income.

Although the steps for starting a private practice are fairly linear, there are countless ways to grow a company. Private practitioners can use a variety of growth strategies: creating a referral engine, adding additional streams of revenue, setting up systems, and hiring team members. Most clinicians love treating clients, but as your practice grows, you may want to spend less time treating patients and more time running your business.

How to Prepare for Growth

Before you leave your job and go all in on growing your practice, create a private practice growth plan. To make your plan, assess your current situation, your future goals, and the particular growth strategies you want to use to increase your income and impact. Conduct a cost-benefit analysis comparing staying at your current job with transitioning to full-time private practice. Compare your current income to what you'll earn in full-time private practice after paying for insurance, rent, taxes, and other business expenses. Shifting from part-time to full-time can be scary, but at some point you have to say to yourself, "I'm doing this. I've got a plan. I'm going all in." Then, go for it! I have full confidence that you'll make the right choices for yourself, your family, and your community.

Case Study
Meet Tia Javier, MA, CCC-SLP

Tia is a bilingual SLP in Richmond, Virginia. She started her private practice with the goal of serving an underserved population and offers speech and occupational therapy as well as language courses for parents. Only a year and a half after opening her private practice, she's seeing over six hundred clients a month and has billboards and commercials advertising her services. Tia is an example of a fast- growth scenario, and I'm so impressed with what she's created in a relatively short time.

Tia is an alum of The Start Your Private Practice Program™ and The Grow Your Private Practice Program.

To hear Tia's full story, listen to the Private Practice Success Stories podcast, Episode #91, "Taking Control of Her Life and Circumstances." Visit PrivatePracticeBook.com/Resources to listen to this episode and download our podcast playlist.

SUCCESSFUL PRIVATE PRACTICES
don't grow themselves.

JENA H. CASTRO-CASBON, MS CCC-SLP

Decision Time

Do you want to see clients part-time or go all in on your private practice?

☐ Start small and stay small on purpose.

☐ Start small and grow gradually.

☐ Start and grow as quickly as possible.

Takeaways

More and more SLPs and OTs are interested in leaving their jobs and working full-time in private practice. Just as there are many ways to start a private practice, there are also many ways to grow a private practice. For example, some private practitioners grow by hiring; others grow by creating additional income streams such as school contracts, paid presentations, and more. Growing allows you to increase your income and your impact. We support growth-focused private practitioners in The Grow Your Private Practice Program.

Conclusion

In this chapter, I shared the five-step Private Practice Success Path. This simplified process for starting a private practice presents the high-level steps you need to take to get your private practice up and running—even without a business background.

There are many more steps involved in starting a private practice—more than I can cover in this book. The 30-Day Private Practice Checklist is the most popular bonus included with The Start Your Private Practice Program™. *We have a special offer for readers of this book* available at <u>PrivatePracticeBook.com/Resources</u>. Visit the link to learn about the special offer and how to get your copy of the 30-Day Private Practice Checklist!

Chapter 4:
The Secrets of Successful Private Practitioners

"Don't wait for your ship to come in. Swim out to it."
—Steve Southerland

Now that you know the simplified way to start a private practice, you may be thinking, "Wow! That sounds easy! Sign me up!"

Since 2008, I've dedicated my life's work to helping SLPs and OTs build private practices in the most efficient and profitable way. The truth is, however, that private practice isn't easy street; otherwise, everyone would do it.

There are tens of thousands of private practitioners who are wildly successful and have six-figure, multi-six-figure, and even million-dollar private practices. (Yes, it's possible!) Many of my successful students have been featured in this book and/or on the Private Practice Success Stories podcast.

However, there are many private practitioners who continue to struggle year after year.

Some private practitioners are able to start and grow their practices quickly and be successful from the very beginning, while others continue to struggle. Why?

Last March, two school OTs chose to start private practices. They were determined to start seeing clients in the spring, aiming to build their private practices to a point at which they could comfortably transition to full-time private practice. They were both excellent OTs, well-regarded by their colleagues. Both had been practicing for ten years and had been interested in private practice for a long time. They both had supportive partners who encouraged them to follow their private practice dreams.

When it came time to start their practices, they both did their market research and determined that there was a need for their services. They worked with the same client population in cities of similar sizes and socioeconomic makeup. They carved out time after work and on Saturday mornings to see clients. They were excited to bring much needed services to their communities and earn extra income for their families. Both took action and started marketing their practices.

Up until that point, they had both done everything correctly. However, one OT successfully acquired twenty-five clients by summertime and was able to leave her job. The other was still struggling to get her first client and, consequently, wasn't able to leave her job.

What was the difference?

Over time, I've come to understand the differences between those who are successful and those who struggle, and it has nothing to do with clinical skills, desire, or whether they have a business background.

It has everything to do with mindset.

I can teach anyone the steps to start a private practice. As a private practice consultant, I've taught thousands of wonderful clinicians how to start and grow successful private practices. But knowing the steps alone won't make you successful.

Success doesn't come from knowing what to *do*—it comes from knowing how to *think*.

In graduate school, as you learned how to be an SLP or OT, you took classes and had placements and clinical experiences that didn't just teach you how to *be* a clinician—they also taught you how to *think* like a clinician.

Just as you learned how to think like a *clinician*, you can learn to think like a *business owner*.

How Helping Professionals Can Become Heart-Led Business Owners

Have you ever thought to yourself, "I'm a helping-people person, not a business person." To be honest, I used to think that way, too.

When I was applying for graduate school for speech-language pathology, my dad planted a seed, telling me, "Maybe one day you'll have a private practice." He's a businessman, and he really wanted me to go into business. But I wasn't interested.

I remember telling him, "Dad, I'm a helping-people person, not a business person. Business is boring, and I'm not all about the money. I just want to help people."

He saw business differently—as a way to earn more while helping more people. He encouraged me to embrace the "and"—that is, to be a clinician *and* a business owner.

In communities across the US and abroad, there aren't enough business owners who truly care about people or about making a difference in their communities. If you start a private practice, you could make a huge difference in your community.

In the previous chapter, I covered the major steps to follow in starting a private practice. Knowing these steps is important, but knowing how to navigate roadblocks between the steps is critical. I plan to help you be successful from the very beginning by teaching you how successful private practitioners think.

How to Break Free from Analysis Paralysis and Move Forward toward Your Goals

"Perfectionism is a form of procrastination."
—Brené Brown

There are many challenges that will inevitably arise when you open a private practice. There are always some external factors you can't control—pandemics, natural disasters, and so forth. There are also some obstacles that come from within you. You can get in your own way, even before you've taken the first step. Does that sound strange?

Consider this:

One day I was waiting in line at the grocery store when I got a text message from a friend—"I've been thinking about starting a private practice for years, but I just keep stopping myself."

I replied, "Why do you think that is?"

She said, "I'm not sure. I just keep overanalyzing everything." I asked, "What is one thing you're stuck on?"

After a few minutes, she replied, "I'm not sure how to hire people."

I was a little confused and scrolled back up the message to see if she had said that she was growing a private practice, not starting one. From our previous messages, it looked like she was still in the beginner stage and hadn't started yet.

So, I asked a question to clarify, "How many clients do you have?" She promptly replied, "Zero."

"Zero," I thought.

That gave me a lot of insight into why she was stuck. She was worrying about issues and decisions that she wouldn't face for months or even years to come. She was putting the cart waaaaaaaaay before the horse. This is a classic example of someone who's stuck in analysis paralysis.

What is Analysis Paralysis?

Analysis paralysis is the inability to make a decision due to overthinking a problem.[1] This results in endless weighing of the pros and cons of various options and struggling to make a decision.

I see analysis paralysis all the time. SLPs and OTs stop themselves from starting or growing their practices by fretting over decisions, big and small. They're so afraid to make mistakes that they try to plan for every single contingency from the start. But if thinking about what might happen ten steps down the road prevents you from taking the first step, you're never going to take the first step.

Having noted my friend's analysis paralysis, I tried to redirect her focus. I said, "How about I help you take care of the steps you need to follow to protect your practice and get your first clients? Then we can figure out hiring."

"Okay," she said. "I tend to overthink things, but I will join your program."

I sent her the link and she joined. A few months later, she still didn't have her first client. While this isn't necessarily a problem, most of our students get their first client within a few weeks of working through the modules in The Start Your Private Practice Program™. We know this because our program manager tracks these data, which we use to monitor student success. Sometimes life events keep people from taking action (pregnancy, illness, moving, etc.), but I wanted to check in on her anyway. I quickly figured out the problem.

"I'm working my way through Module 2," she told me. "And I don't have a client yet because I still have so many questions."

"Have you asked questions in the private student group so the mentors can support you?"

"I've asked a few questions, and they responded. But I'm still not sure how to proceed on a few things."

"I understand. You have all the information you need to get started successfully. But at some point, you have to take action. This is a 'You can lead a horse to water, but you can't make him drink' situation."

"You're right."

I don't know if she ever got her first client. Her analysis paralysis got in the way of her success. If she had started years ago when she first considered the idea, just think how many clients she would have been able to help and how much extra income she could have generated for her family. *Analysis paralysis was literally costing her money.*

It's not good to make impulsive decisions about your practice, but in order to have a successful practice, you need to make decisions that move your company forward.

Struggling private practitioners let roadblocks, big or small, stop them in their tracks. Successful private practitioners see roadblocks and quickly find ways to go around them.

Why SLPs and OTs Are So Susceptible to Analysis Paralysis

SLPs and OTs are particularly susceptible to analysis paralysis, for a few reasons.

First, we're smart! We're critical thinkers who know how to analyze things. Graduate school and clinical practice are all about analyzing and synthesizing information so that we can make the best decisions for our clients.

Another reason why SLPs and OTs are susceptible to analysis paralysis is because we tend to be risk averse and worry about making "wrong" decisions. After all, a mistake can negatively affect a client. But making mistakes is part of life and integral to learning. Being informed is the best way to reduce your chances of making a mistake. But at some point, you have to move forward with the best solution you've come up with.

Actually, you've already learned how to move past analysis paralysis. Think back to your early clinical practice, when you weren't sure how to interpret a diagnostic score or pick which treatment approach to use with a new client. You knew your client was depending on you to make a decision for them, so you used the information you had to make the most informed decision you could. If you tried something and it didn't work as expected, you reevaluated the decision and changed course. *You can do the same thing with your business.*

What Happens if You Don't Move Past Analysis Paralysis?

It's easy to get stuck in analysis paralysis when you're considering a decision you've never faced before and you don't feel equipped to make it. For example, one of the first decisions you have to make as a private practitioner is how much to charge for your services. That's a big decision!

Here are some common questions that people have when thinking about their private pay rate:

- How much should I charge?
- How much are other people charging?
- What are people in my area able to afford?
- How will I collect payment?
- Should I bill them at the time of the session or send an invoice?
- If I send out invoices, should I do it weekly or monthly?
- What HIPAA compliant platforms are available?
- Should I accept insurance?

You may not have answers for all these questions. Some people agonize over the answers to these questions for years. Years! These are the kinds of questions we support our students with on a daily basis.

Imagine that you spent the last two years worrying about whether you should charge $100 per session or $80 per session. You've been losing money! If you had chosen to charge $80 and had only three sessions per week, you would have earned $24,960 over that time period.

2 years × 3 clients at $80 per hour = $24,960
Being stuck in analysis paralysis is expensive!

The lesson here? Make the best decision you can with the information you have, and then move on. Nine times out of ten, it'll be fine. Almost all mistakes can be fixed later—just like when a treatment approach doesn't work out as planned.

Case Study
Meet Rene Robles, MS, CCC-SLP, and Cristina Ramos, MS, CCC-SLP

Rene and Cristina are private practice partners who run Five Oaks Speech Therapy Services in California. They had a dream of opening five brick-and-mortar locations within five years. (That's right, five clinics in five years! And guess what? They did it!) When the pandemic hit, they scrambled to make some quick decisions to keep their private practice afloat. They had to choose a telepractice platform in order to continue serving their clients and to make sure their employees got paid. They didn't waste time agonizing over small differences between companies/platforms; they picked one quickly and moved forward.

To hear Rene and Cristina's full story, listen to the Private Practice Success Stories podcast, Episode #70, "Five Clinics in Five Years." Visit PrivatePracticeBook.com/Resources to listen to this episode and download our podcast playlist.

When you're starting and growing a private practice, it's natural to face roadblocks. How you handle them will determine how successful you become.

WHEN YOU'RE STUCK, YOU'RE NOT HELPING ANYONE. IF YOU WANT TO HELP PEOPLE, GET UNSTUCK AND

move forward.

JENA H. CASTRO-CASBON, MS CCC-SLP

Takeaways

Analysis paralysis is normal, especially when you're facing new decisions.

When you're starting (or growing) a private practice, you'll face unexpected roadblocks. You can let them stop you, or you can work through them. If you're stuck, you're not helping others or yourself. Action is the best way to help people. Thinking and over-thinking don't help you reach your goals— action does. So, make the best decision you can and move forward toward your goals.

You've got this!

How to Invest in Yourself and Transform Your Life

"The best gift you can give to yourself is to invest in yourself."
–Pooja Agnihotri

"I guess I'm doing this," I told my mom.

"You're doing it! I am so proud of you. This is truly what you're meant to do."

As I submitted the deposit for graduate school, I was excited about my future, but nervous too. I entered my Master's in Communication Disorders program without an undergraduate background. My only experience in the field included shadowing a few SLPs and reading an introductory communication disorders textbook. I decided to move to Boston and invest my time and money in graduate school because I wanted to be an SLP, and the only way to become one was to invest in a master's degree.

What is Investing?

Investing is when you pay a sum of money now for the opportunity to have more money later. Most people are familiar with investing in the stock market or real estate. Even if you don't understand the inner workings of investments, you understand the process of investing a smaller amount of money now so that you have more money later.

When you invested in graduate school, you paid a large sum of money (and potentially had to take out loans) in order to acquire the knowledge, skills, and credentials to be a licensed professional and earn a certain salary.

You may feel like graduate school was an excellent investment, and perhaps you would make the same investment decision again. Or you may feel that although you love your profession, the return on investment (ROI) wasn't as high as you would have liked, given your current earnings.

SLPs and OTs are used to investing time and money in things they care about.

- We invested in graduate school to become SLPs and OTs.
- We invest in educational opportunities for our children.
- We invest in gym memberships to improve our health.

- We invest in date nights with our partners to keep our relationships strong.
- We invest in travel in order to have enriching experiences.

The investments don't stop there. After you invested in your degree, you also invested money and time in continuing education in order to become a better therapist. Many of us struggle with insecurity about whether we're good therapists, so we tend to overcompensate by loading up on continuing education.

I did an informal poll in the SLP and OT Private Practice Beginners Facebook group and asked, "How much money have you spent on continuing education over the course of your career?"

Here are some of the responses:

- "Thousands."
- "Too much."
- "At least $3,000 (and I have the continuing education certificates to prove it!)."
- "More than I can count."
- "$10,000+."
- "I should have gotten a PhD."

We are so dedicated to our clients. We want to provide the best services possible, which often means taking many courses on our clinical interests so that we have a deep knowledge and understanding of how to help our clients. SLPs and OTs thoroughly understand that becoming really good at something—like being a top-notch therapist—costs time and money.

And yet when it comes to investing in business education and business expenses, some private practitioners hesitate, while others understand the value of investing in solutions that save time and money.

Case Study
Meet Samantha Asher, MA, CCC-SLP

Samantha Asher is a private practitioner in Deerfield, Illinois. She created a private practice schedule that allows her to make a six-figure salary while working three days a week. The days she works are long days, but her schedule allows her to have Mondays and Fridays off with her children so she can do things like go to toddler ballet and library story time. Because she designed her private practice this way, she is able to support her family financially and also be there for her kids' adventures. Samantha accepts private pay, health savings accounts (HSAs), and several insurance plans.

Samantha is an alum of The Start Your Private Practice Program™ and The Grow Your Private Practice Program.

To hear Samantha's full story, listen to the Private Practice Success Stories podcast, Episode #167, "Building a Six-Figure Private Practice in Less than 2 Years." Visit PrivatePracticeBook.com/Resources to listen to this episode and download our podcast playlist.

If You're Going to Start a Business, Learn How to Run It Well

We went to graduate school to learn how to be clinicians. If we wanted to be business owners, we would have gone to business school. But now, you're interested in starting a private practice—which is a business.

It's just as it is important to gain clinical knowledge in order to successfully work with clients; it's important to gain business knowledge in order to be a successful business owner.

The good news is that you don't have to go to business school or get an MBA. However, you do need to invest time and money in at least a basic business education as part of your private practice journey.

There are a lot of misconceptions about business education. A lot of clinicians think that business is boring, hard, or confusing, and worry that they don't have a business mind. But just as you developed a clinical mind, *you can develop a business mind.*

I've been helping people start and grow private practices since 2008. I've seen many practices succeed, and I've also seen many practices struggle. One of the key differences is whether a practitioner is willing to go the extra mile to develop business skills specific to SLP and OT private practice so they can run a successful business.

As the saying goes, "You don't know what you don't know."

If you're going to run a business, you need to know how to run it effectively and profitably so you don't have expensive surprises. Those who are willing to invest time and money in developing skills in marketing, finances, and leadership and who set up systems to work smarter fare much better than those who aren't willing to do so.

It's not just business *education* that SLPs and OTs shy away from. Many private practitioners hesitate to *invest* in their businesses—that is, to invest in marketing, hiring, or software [e.g., electronic medical record (EMR) systems]—out of fear that they will lose money.

- "I want to use an EMR system, but it costs $50 per month. I can't afford that."
- "I want to hire a biller, but they'll take 6% of my revenue."
- "I want to join a business education program, but it's a lot of money."

Remember, investments are designed to make you money. When you're first getting started and don't have many clients, $50 a month for an EMR system seems like a lot. But consider this—

the features available in the EMR system will save you time, which means you'll make more money. In that light, the EMR system is worth the expense. Many EMR software companies offer appointment reminders for clients. Sure, you're paying $50 a month for the software, but appointment reminders can help bring thousands of dollars into your practice by increasing your attendance rate; therefore, the EMR system will easily pay for itself.

Some private practices opt to hire billers to help them collect payments. Billers often work for either for a flat fee or for a percentage of the income they bring in, usually 5%–10%. Depending on how many sessions your practice is conducting, 5%–10% may be a big expense. But, if you drop the ball on billing, forget to send invoices, use incorrect codes and get rejected by insurance, and so forth—all these things cost you money. In that case, it's worth it to pay 5%–10% to ensure you receive the money you're earning instead of losing out on payments by not sending invoices or billing correctly. When your private practice grows, you can hire an employee to do your billing in-house, which will save you even more money if you have enough claims.

Struggling private practitioners choose not to invest in themselves or their businesses out of fear of loss.

Successful private practitioners choose to invest in themselves and their businesses in order to gain.

When you have the opportunity to invest in a solution, calculate the return on your investment. If paying for a course, certification, EMR system, website, or billing service helps you make money or saves you time, then the investment is probably worth it. Time is money. Don't waste it.

If you invest in something and it doesn't work out, you learned a lesson. Investments are not guaranteed. But not investing in time- and money-saving strategies makes it harder to grow your practice.

When I first started my private practice, I invested in business cards. When they came in the mail, I was so proud of them. They made my private practice feel so official. I couldn't wait to hand them out and start getting clients from them. But that didn't happen. Why? *Because I never handed them out.* I carried them with me in my bag, but I mostly put them in fish bowls at restaurants to try to win free lunches.

I never placed myself in situations where I could give them to someone who could become a referral source. When I did have opportunities to pass out my cards, I got nervous and held back.

Investing in business cards didn't work because I didn't put in any effort. However, buying business cards taught me a huge lesson. My personality is much more suited to advertising through a website than through business cards. So, my next investment was a website; through the website, my private practice grew.

What Happens If You Don't Fully Invest in Your Business?

Private practitioners who are willing to invest money and time into learning how to run their businesses (marketing, systems, finances, leadership) will get a lot farther a lot faster than those who don't. Smart investments with great returns are shortcuts for success. You have to be willing to spend time and money up front, but these kinds of investments put you in a position to gain more in the future.

Many private practitioners are only willing to invest in partial solutions. For example, they realize that they want to learn more about business, so they take a general business course at a local community college. General courses are just that—general. General business courses are often not directly applicable to SLP and OT private practice. To use the information you gain from them, you need to put in time and effort to connect the dots to SLP and OT private practice!

You don't have time to sift through general information and connect the dots. You need specific and actionable content that you can put into practice and that generates results almost immediately.

Investing in general information and partial solutions is often a waste of time and money and won't solve problems specific to your private practice. It's worth it to invest in tried and true strategies specific to your industry.

How to Move Past the Fear of Investing in Yourself

If you have an opportunity to invest in your private practice through business education or in some other way and you're nervous about doing so, try doing the following:

- Calculate the potential return on investment. Sit down with a calculator and a sheet of paper and figure out what the potential return on your investment is.
- If it's a potential money maker, calculate the amount of money you stand to earn (not just immediately, but over time).
- If it's a potential time saver, calculate the amount of time you could save.
- Think about the long-term professional and personal gains (money earned over time, time saved that you can spend with your family).
- If you choose to invest, keep your receipt, because business expenses are tax deductible.

Investments often have an up-front cost in terms of money and time. For example, starting a private practice on the side will give you a busier-than-usual schedule at first. There is no denying that. But if your goal is to build up your private practice income so you can leave your job and work part-time hours, then you may want to sacrifice time now in order to have a more flexible schedule later.

Challenge yourself to recoup your investments as quickly as possible.

Any time I invest in business courses, coaching, marketing, and so forth, I always challenge myself to obtain the return on my investment as quickly as possible. After I reach that point, all the money I earn or time I save feels free.

INVEST IN YOURSELF. YOU AND YOUR FUTURE ARE
worth investing in.

JENA H. CASTRO-CASBON, MS CCC-SLP

Takeaways

Learning to be a business owner means learning to think like a business owner. When business owners have an opportunity to learn something new or implement a new strategy, they don't think about the cost (what they will lose)—they think about the return (what they will gain).

In your private practice journey, you'll have the option to invest in all sorts of things. Shift your thinking from "What will this cost me?" to "What will this get me?" When you invest in something, work hard to make back your investment as quickly as possible; everything earned thereafter will feel like a bonus.

How to Get Over Guilt and Charge for Your Services

"You are generous enough. Stop giving away your time, effort, and labor and start building real wealth."
—Rachel Rodgers

SLPs and OTs have advanced degrees. We invest in countless continuing education courses. We practice our craft daily and help hundreds and even thousands of people live fuller and more independent lives. We put our heart and soul into our work and are proud of the difference we make in the lives of our clients.

So why do so many of us feel guilty charging for private therapy services? Let's discuss why this is and, more importantly, what we can do about it.

In traditional employment settings, such as school and hospital systems, we often try to negotiate for higher salaries when applying for jobs. Once we're in those jobs, raises and bonuses are rare. Many clinicians leave traditional jobs like these in order to earn more money. But when SLPs and OTs are in private practice and finally have control over their salaries, many report feeling guilty accepting payments from clients.

What's the difference? SLPs and OTs don't feel nearly as guilty accepting money from school or hospital systems as they do accepting money from individuals.

What Is Guilt, and What Causes It?

It is completely normal to have feelings of guilt from time to time. Sometimes guilt is appropriate—for instance, the guilt someone feels after committing a crime. Other times, people feel inappropriately guilty over things that are out of their control, often based on assumptions regarding how others feel. Inappropriate guilt can lead to anxiety, stress, and depression.

Why Private Practitioners Feel Guilty Charging for Services

Women and helping professionals are more susceptible than others to inappropriate feelings of guilt that get in the way of their personal relationships and professional success. Those who pursue the SLP and OT fields tend to be women who consider themselves helping-people persons; many of them think that taking money from clients means they are harming, not helping. SLPs and OTs say things like, "I didn't choose this profession for the money"; this kind of comment excuses institutions from paying us more and makes clinicians who desire more money feel guilty. Money guilt then gets in the way of their growth and success.

In the SLP and OT Private Practice Beginners Facebook group, there is a lot of talk about feeling guilty for charging clients. People say things like:

- "I worry that families can't afford my services, and I don't want to put them out."
- "I worry that my clinical skills aren't good enough."
- "People have a lot of other services to pay for."

As an SLP or OT, you need to recognize that the financial situation of your clients is (1) not your fault and (2) not your business.

Undercharging Leads to Underearning

Many private practitioners undercharge for their services because they feel guilty.

Consider Sally and Renee, two hypothetical private practitioners with similar backgrounds and skill levels. Sally charges $80 per session because she feels guilty charging more. Renee feels confident about her pricing and charges $125 per session. If both private practitioners conduct twenty sessions per week over the course of a year, Sally's gross revenue is $83,200, and Renee's gross revenue is

$130,000. That's a difference of almost $50,000!

In addition to undercharging, some private practitioners "forget" to send invoices or don't follow up on late payments because they feel guilty; this further impacts their earnings and stress levels. Guilt doesn't pay the bills.

It's worthwhile to examine and shift your money beliefs in order to take care of the financial health of your practice. More money needs to make its way into the hands of good people who can make a positive difference in the world—that includes you!

Struggling private practitioners want to help everyone and feel badly if someone can't afford their services. This leads them to undercharge for their services and overbook their time to make up the difference.

Successful private practitioners know that they can't help *everyone*. They offer services and payer sources that they have confidence in, knowing that their ideal clients will hire them.

Seven Reasons to Feel Good About Earning Money in Your Practice

Feelings of guilt may come up from time to time, but you can choose how you react to them. Here are seven ways to reframe your thoughts about earning money as a private practitioner.

1. You're Being Paid for Your Career Experience, Not Just the Session

When you hire a professional, such as a hairstylist, mechanic, or plumber, you pay for their time—but the real value is in their expertise. They earned their expertise through training programs and on the job, just like you have. People pay you for your years of experience, not the minutes of each session.

2. Money Helps You Have Less Financial Stress, Which Helps You Concentrate on Your Clients

Financial stress is a huge burden and is very distracting. If you're worried about finances as you're with a client, it draws your attention away from the client.

3. Money Helps You Pay Back the Student Loans for Your Degree

The average ASHA-certified SLP accrues more than $53,000 in student loan debt[2] that can take decades to pay off. Using the knowledge you gained in school to earn money through private practice helps pay off your student loans. Without that knowledge, you wouldn't be able to help your clients.

4. Money Is a Reward for Your Hard Work

Having more money allows you to live the life you've imagined for yourself and your family. You work hard as a private practitioner; having additional money allows you to do fun things with your family, save up for big-ticket items, go on trips, or retire early.

5. Money Helps You Afford to Take Breaks and Refresh

I'm sure you've heard the saying, "You can't pour from an empty cup." If you burn out, you can't help anyone. Having enough money allows you to take time off to rest and relax, preventing burnout.

6. The More Money You Earn, the More You Can Give

Money makes you more of who you already are. If you're a kind and generous person—like most SLPs and OTs—you'll be able to be even more kind and generous. Having more money allows you to donate to charities, community organizations, tee ball teams, and so forth. It also enables you to give bonuses to your employees.

7. Making Money Helps You Keep Your Practice Open and Allows You to Expand Services So You Can Help More People

Private practices need cash flow and profits to stay in business. Some practices aren't profitable because their expenses exceed their revenue. Others aren't profitable because they undercharge. If you don't earn enough, you'll have to close your practice. Then you won't be able to help anyone.

Takeaways

Exploring and changing your beliefs regarding money is essential to your short- and long-term success in private practice. When feelings of guilt arise, how you react to them is your choice. You can choose to feel guilty or choose not to feel guilty. Your session fee and the payer sources you accept may not fit the needs of every client, and that's okay.

Your private practice isn't for everyone, and you shouldn't contort yourself to make others comfortable at your own expense. You have an advanced degree and the knowledge and skills that go with it. It's time to proudly earn as a clinician and business owner and let go of the guilt.

How to Let Go of Imposter Syndrome and Start Your Private Practice

"Here's the thing that's really sad: Imposter syndrome doesn't just make you feel shitty about yourself; it also keeps you broke."
—Rachel Rodgers

It was late December. I was scrolling on social media late at night and saw a social media post that changed my life.

Prior to this, I was very susceptible to imposter syndrome. I would get an idea about a new service or offer and a little voice inside my brain would say terrible things like:

- "Are you really qualified to do that?"
- "Who are you to do that?"
- "Why should anyone listen to you?"

All these thoughts were imposter syndrome rearing its ugly head. What did the life-changing social media post say?

It said: "What are you going to leave behind in the new year?"

Immediately, I thought: "Imposter syndrome. That's what I'm leaving behind."

And that, honestly, is all it took for me to move past it. You can leave imposter syndrome behind, too!

What Is Imposter Syndrome?

Imposter syndrome is a phenomenon that causes qualified people to doubt their own abilities despite evidence of their accomplishments. It is most common in high-achieving women, and it's very common in SLPs and OTs.[3]

Why SLPs and OTs Are So Susceptible to Imposter Syndrome

Do you feel like imposter syndrome is something that has prevented you from starting a private practice? When it comes to starting a private practice, it's very common to worry:

- "I don't know enough."
- "I'm not qualified."
- "I'm not ready."
- "What will people think?"

However, you have an advanced degree. You completed a clinical fellowship (SLPs). You have a state license and a certificate of clinical competence from ASHA (SLPs). You've invested in continuing education, and you practice your craft every day. Your experience and expertise are enough for someone to have considered you qualified and hired you as an employee.

The SLP and OT fields are susceptible to imposter syndrome because they're vast, and there's a lot to know. In addition, as you run the gauntlet of **getting your degree and certifications and starting your career,** other people decide when you're qualified. Educators, mentors, and committee members are constantly deciding your fate in the field. Consequently, if you're thinking about private practice, you might be waiting for someone to tell you that you're qualified and ready.

Take it from me:

- If you've completed the foregoing steps and have something to bring to the table in terms of value, you're qualified!
- Your clinical skills are valuable—money valuable. Let them be valued.

Struggling private practitioners let imposter syndrome stop them from putting themselves out there because of fear of judgment.

Successful private practitioners ignore imposter syndrome and put themselves out there, knowing that clients need them.

What Happens if You Don't Move Past Imposter Syndrome

When you choose not to move past imposter syndrome and let it keep you at your current level, you won't be able to serve others (or yourself) at a higher level. You'll keep playing small and be stuck in situations that don't serve you (or others). For example, maybe you're stuck in a hospital or school system that isn't set up for you or your clients to be successful. If you let imposter syndrome hold you back from opportunities to work with private clients, you'll miss out on helping people and earning income for your family.

If you're stuck on the hamster wheel of pursuing continuing education credits in order to feel qualified to start a private practice, you probably have a million continuing education awards but still don't feel qualified enough to start a private practice because of a lack of business education. Gathering information without taking action doesn't help you feel qualified, it helps you feel overwhelmed.

At some point, you have to decide that you're qualified enough to take the next step. I turned down three opportunities to see private clients before I finally said, "Yes!" If you've passed on chances to see private clients and want to be able to seize the opportunity next time, start getting your ducks in a row and kick imposter syndrome to the curb when it appears.

How to Move Past Imposter Syndrome

Imposter syndrome isn't a disease that you can cure. It's a misrepresentation of yourself and your skills. Imposter syndrome creeps in when you're on the cusp of a big leap forward or about to step outside your comfort zone. It holds you back. Letting imposter syndrome win means staying safe in your comfort zone.

When it does present itself (and it will), acknowledge it, and then roll your eyes and say: "You, again," in a disgusted voice.

Then continue: "You're not welcome here. Go away. You want to keep me stuck, but I won't let you. If I let you keep me stuck, I won't be able to help anyone. I see you, but I'm ignoring you. Goodbye."

Imposter syndrome will go away for a while and then return as you get ready to take another step outside your comfort zone. Repeat the above conversation. Don't let imposter syndrome hold you back!

When people tell me that imposter syndrome is the reason why they haven't started their private practices, I often ask them, "Has anyone encouraged you to start a practice?" Nine times out of ten, they say something along the lines of, "Yes! My spouse/parent/sibling/best friend has been telling me to do this for years."

If someone in your life has been encouraging you to start your practice:

1. They sound like a keeper.
2. They know you've spent a lot of time and money becoming an SLP or OT, and they want to see you happy in your career.
3. They see potential in you that you don't see yet.

If someone is discouraging you from private practice, but it's something that you want to do, go for it and prove them wrong.

If you don't have someone rooting for you, I'm happy to be your number one cheerleader. Stop letting imposter syndrome prevent you from following your dreams.

IMPOSTER SYNDROME WANTS TO STOP YOU FROM HELPING PEOPLE.

Don't let it.

JENA H. CASTRO-CASBON, MS CCC-SLP

Takeaways

Imposter syndrome will come up from time to time. Now, however, you know that you can choose how to react to it. If you let it stop you from building your private practice, you won't be able to help people, which was your motivation for becoming an SLP or OT. Imposter syndrome loves to prey on people who are struggling with private practice. It gets into your head and says terrible things, trying to stop you from moving forward.

Don't think that successful private practitioners never feel imposter syndrome. They do. But they choose to ignore it and don't let it stop them.

Leave imposter syndrome behind. It's not helping you or anyone else.

How to Feel Fear and Do It Anyway

"Fear has a very concrete power of keeping us from doing and saying the things that are our purpose."
—Luvvie Ajayi Jones

"Do you treat private clients?" the woman asked, with hopeful curiosity.

Time froze. This was the question I had been waiting for. I wanted to say "Yes!" with every fiber of my being. I had the dream and the desire, but not the confidence. (Yet!)

It had been a few weeks since my coworkers had asked me if I wanted to start working with private clients. They helped me get set up to see clients.

Right after Christmas, I was heading home from work when my dad called and asked, "What did you get for your Christmas bonus?" It felt like a punch to the gut.

"Nothing."

"Nothing?" he asked in surprise.

"Nothing. I don't think they do bonuses here."

He was shocked. My dad works for a large company and is used to getting a Christmas bonus. He was sad to hear that I wasn't getting one. And to be honest, I was too. Sarah and I were getting married in September of the following year, and we could have used some extra money for our wedding fund. I was new to being an SLP and didn't realize that clinicians rarely get bonuses:

- No matter how hard we work for our clients (on behalf of our employers)
- No matter our level of expertise
- No matter how much we care about the people we serve

I was lucky to have mentors that helped me get set up for private practice. Without them, I wouldn't have had the confidence to start when the right first client came along.

A few weeks later, a prospective client asked, "Do you treat private clients?"

My future flashed before my eyes. Fear started to bubble up and take over, but this time I didn't let it. I had already turned down at least three people. I knew that if fear kept me from seizing these opportunities, I would never start a private practice. Instead of looking at all the things that might go wrong, I looked into the future and saw all the things that were waiting on the other side of fear.

- I would be working with clients I loved, and my career satisfaction would return.
- I would be earning extra money for my wedding and would have enough additional income to start paying off student loans and saving for a house.
- I would have a flexible schedule when we had children.

I decided to push fear to the side, take a deep breath, and say, "Yes. I see private clients." At that moment, I felt the fear, but I accepted the client anyway. I wasn't just saying yes to that client—I was saying yes to myself, my family, my community, and my future.

I was afraid that everything I had lined up for starting a private practice would suddenly dissipate. But instead of staying in a place of fear, I took action. I took on my first client and discovered that private practice wasn't as scary as I thought. I was scared to set a rate for my services because I was afraid that the client would say no. I was worried about where my first client would come from. I was intimidated because I was young and I wondered if people would take me seriously.

I didn't get a bonus from my employer that year, but by the time I got married, I had earned an extra

$24,000 on the side by seeing private clients. It was far more than any bonus or raise that my employer might have given me. I was no longer afraid; I was exhilarated by seeing private clients. I was no longer letting short-term fear stand between me and my future. I was proud of what I had accomplished and excited for what was to come.

What Is Fear?

Fear is an unpleasant, often strong emotion caused by anticipation or awareness of danger. Fear is designed to keep us safe from dangers like falling off a cliff, stepping into traffic, or getting hurt. But sometimes fear stops us from doing things that aren't dangerous—things that are just new and unknown.

Struggling private practitioners see difficulties as failure, proof that they won't make it. Successful private practitioners won't accept failure as an option and push through fear.

The only way you can fail is to give up. If your private practice is struggling to get more clients, you haven't failed. You just haven't yet found a marketing approach that works for you.

Why SLPs and OTs Are So Susceptible to Fear

SLPs and OTs are susceptible to being afraid of things they've never done. Clinicians like to feel confident in their knowledge, and they worry about making mistakes or missing steps. Any time you do something you've never done before, there is likely to be some level of fear.

When I talk to SLPs and OTs who are thinking about starting private practices, they often list fear of failure as something that stops them.

Failure means different things to different people, so I ask people to tell me what failure looks like.

- If you're afraid of getting sued, there are specific ways to protect yourself from lawsuits (professional liability insurance, completing clinical documentation, following the code of ethics).

- If you're afraid of not making enough money, keep your full-time job while building your private practice.

The main way to prevent your private practice from failing (from a financial point of view) is to keep it profitable by making sure that your income exceeds your expenses.

What Happens if You Don't Move Past Fear

If you try private practice and it doesn't work out (i.e., you're not making enough money or you don't like it), you can always go back to work in a school or hospital. You have a safety net, because the SLP and OT professions are in such high demand. But if you want to have a private practice (even a small one), you owe it to yourself, your family, and your future clients to try it out.

How Can You Move Past Fear?

If you're interested in starting a private practice but have some level of trepidation, the best way to move past the fear is to take baby steps. Combat fear of the unknown by educating yourself about what you're trying to accomplish.

For example, if you were going on a trip to a new place, you'd probably do the following things before you leave:
- Research what to expect (what to do and what to avoid)
- Ask advice from people who have already been there
- Plan out what you want to do

Travelers understand that sometimes the best laid plans don't go as anticipated, but they trust that they'll be able to figure things out. The same goes for private practice.

In graduate school, SLPs and OTs are mentored by supervisors and clinical instructors. Your supervisors and clinical instructors showed you the professional ropes and taught you shortcuts. Without their mentorship, you would have had book knowledge without practical knowledge. In a similar vein, a private practice mentor can help you learn the ropes of private practice, beyond basic knowledge.

Before you start your private practice, gather information about what to do and what to expect, but don't underestimate the value of mentorship. Ongoing support from people who have already experienced private practice (i.e., mentors) will help you cut the learning curve.

Mentorship is extremely valuable. Mentors share their journeys and give tips and shortcuts to success. Their generosity and commitment to the next generation is wonderful and often hard to find. A mentor can save you years of struggle by telling you what to focus on and when. Mentees who benefit from solid mentorship have higher success rates than those who don't have mentors.[4] Because of the value that mentorship provides, ongoing mentorship is often paid.

I understand the value of paid mentorship, which is why students in my programs get access to private practice mentors that help set them up for success. I pay an entire team of mentors on your behalf so you don't have to go through the trouble of finding and paying a mentor.

Can You Find Free Mentors?

It's hard to find free mentors. Most private practitioners are pretty busy. Although someone may support you at arm's length, they probably won't let you pick their brain if you're starting a practice that will compete with them. I've had wonderful mentors in my life (most of them paid), and they were worth their weight in gold. Not only did they help me know what to do (and in what order), they listened to my fears and hesitations and helped me move beyond them to the success that awaited me on the other side. That's why I'm committed to offering mentorship as part of my paid programs. The private practitioners who serve as mentors for my programs are amazing people who are extremely knowledgeable and committed to helping the next generation of private practitioners. And because the students in our programs are from many different places, the mentors aren't hesitant when people want to pick their brains. They gladly share what they know in order to help our students.

The first step in moving past fear is to arm yourself with knowledge.

The second step is to listen to and learn from those who have already navigated the path you're on and want to help you succeed.

JUST BECAUSE YOU'RE STRUGGLING DOESN'T MEAN *you're failing*.

JENA H. CASTRO-CASBON, MS CCC-SLP

Takeaways

Doing new things can be scary. Starting graduate school was scary. Starting my clinical fellowship was scary. Starting my private practice was scary. Writing and releasing this book was scary. But you know what? It was worth it.

If private practice was easy, everyone would do it. Stop fearing what could go wrong, and start welcoming what could go right. It's perfectly normal to feel afraid when you face new challenges. The trick is to feel the fear, arm yourself with knowledge, and then move forward in spite of the fear.

> *"Whether you think you can or you can't, you're right."*
> **—Henry Ford**

The Top Predictor of Success in Private Practice

I'll share another personal story to reinforce what we've learned so far. I have been overweight for pretty much my whole life. I've tried diet after diet. I've signed up for weight loss programs more times than I can count, and I've ended up canceling every time.

Who was at fault? The diet programs? No. Was it my fault? Yes. Why? Because I wasn't committed.

I'm going to say that again, because it's important. I wasn't committed.

Commitment is essential to success. You need to make an initial commitment, but you also need to recommit when things get challenging. I've committed to health and weight loss, and I've recommitted to health and weight loss when I've skipped the gym or eaten things I shouldn't have. Commitment got me started. *Recommitment keeps me moving toward my health goals.*

The same thing goes for your private practice. In order to be successful in private practice you need to commit to doing it (even part-time or on the side) and then recommit to it when you come up against a roadblock. Fear will convince you that there are reasons why you shouldn't start a private practice, but I hope this book has presented many more reasons why you should.

I can give you all the steps to get started, but your mindset will determine whether you have a successful private practice or a struggling one.

You can commit to being successful, or you can commit to continuing to struggle.

You can start a private practice, just like tens of thousands of SLPs and OTs before you. If you know you want to be in private practice for the freedom, flexibility, and financial independence it offers and you're ready to take control of your professional, personal, and financial life, then it's time to start your practice. Armed with the information you've learned so far and the mindset shifts that you're starting to make, you're ready to get set up to see private clients.

The last chapter of this book may lead to the next chapter of your life. Keep going!

Chapter 5:
You Can Start a Private Practice

Congratulations on making it to this point in your private practice journey!

You are on your way to being able to make a bigger difference for yourself, your clients, your community, and your own family through your private practice.

I sincerely hope that you've benefited from the information and inspiration in this book. By taking the time to dream about a private practice and making a plan for starting, you have successfully completed Stage 1 of The Start Your Private Practice Program™.

☐ I completed Stage 1 of the Private Practice Journey!

Here's what you've accomplished:

- You learned that SLPs and OTs are joining the Private Practice Movement in order to have more freedom, flexibility, fulfillment, financial independence, family, fun, and future. You identified which of my favorite F words are pulling you toward private practice.

- You completed the Balance Builder, identifying areas of your life that are out of balance, and you're ready to create a plan to have more balance in your life.

- You learned about the New Way to start a private practice, which is much simpler, faster, and cheaper than the Old Way. You know that you can start a private practice at any age without quitting your job, taking on a ton of debt, or saving up thousands of dollars, and that through private practice you can work with ideal clients and have more balance in your life.

- You learned about the Private Practice Success Path. You know that the major steps are to picture, protect, promote, get paid in, and prepare to grow your private practice.

- You learned that the difference between successful private practitioners and struggling private practitioners often comes down to mindset and that in order to be successful in private practice, you have to break free from analysis paralysis, invest in yourself, let go of imposter syndrome, get over feeling guilty about charging for your services, and acknowledge fear but keep moving forward anyway.

As you read through the book and completed the prompts and worksheets, you made your first choices as a private practitioner and business owner.

For example, you answered these questions:

- Why do you want to have a practice?
- Who do you want to help?
- Where will you see your clients?
- What services will you provide?
- When do you want to see your clients?

You're on your way to changing your life, your family life, and the lives of future clients in your community.

You've successfully completed Stage 1: Plan Your Private Practice. Now it's time to move on to Stage 2: Start Your Private Practice.

If you decide to start a private practice and join the Private Practice Movement, your future clients, future self, and community will thank you. Starting a private practice takes time and money. It's an investment in your future that will pay for itself many times over. You can't put a price on having more freedom, flexibility, fulfillment, and financial independence. Neither can you put a price on time spent with family or having fun. You were made for more, and you deserve more. You *can* start a private practice, and I can't wait to see where you go from here.

If you want help implementing what you've learned in this book, consider joining The Start Your Private Practice Program™. As a student, you'll get access step-by-step resources and ongoing support from our team of mentors. Trying to figure out private practice on your own is time-consuming, and you risk making mistakes.

No matter what path you choose, I hope you take concrete steps toward starting rather than being stuck in analysis paralysis, feeling overwhelmed and letting opportunities pass you by. Remember, you don't have to jump into private practice full-time;

you can start a private practice on the side without giving up your steady pay and benefits.

If you're not quite sure yet, listen to episodes of the Private Practice Success Stories podcast. Listen for commonalities between the guests' stories and your story. My guests have had many of the doubts and fears that you have, but they chose to face their fear, to be the change they wanted to see in their lives and careers.

If you choose not to pursue private practice, please pass this book on to an SLP or OT colleague. If you decide later that you're ready to pursue private practice and you want my help to get started, you know where to find me.

You're safe to try private practice.

There are children and adults in your community who are stuck on wait lists and going without services; you can be the answer to their prayers. You don't have to take on debt, loans, or a lot of overhead to start a private practice. You can get started very inexpensively with a handful of clients and grow from there. You can start a private practice with very little up-front investment if you only spend money on required expenses (e.g., essential legal protection).

Starting a private practice isn't as hard as people make it out to be. You can learn all the steps involved and the order in which you need to complete them.

Starting a private practice isn't as overwhelming as it used to be. Using the New Way to start a private practice, you start small and grow. When you're your own boss, you'll be able to make decisions that work best for you and your clients. You'll finally have control over your professional, personal, and financial life.

You don't have to embark on the private practice journey alone. Mentorship and community are essential to your success. It's invaluable to surround yourself with people who are farther along than you are and who want to speed up your learning curve and save you from missteps.

It's important to invest in your business skills in the same way that you invested in clinical skills. You can run a successful business, but you need to learn basic business skills in order to do so.

Burnout won't go away on its own. If you need to get your spark back in order to keep working as an SLP or OT, seeing private clients is an excellent way to do it. Private practitioners prioritize balance over burnout.

My private practice started by accident.

When my dad suggested that maybe one day I'd have a private practice, I shrugged him off, because I thought that business was boring and only for greedy people. I wasn't sure I had what it took to be successful in business. If I had prevented myself from starting a private practice because I didn't feel worthy of being fairly compensated for my time, where would I be now?

Are you preventing yourself from moving forward with private practice despite friends, family, colleagues, and clients nudging you to start?

I started my private practice when I was newly engaged. Prior to meeting Sarah, I was a carefree, single woman. After we met and fell in love, it was clear that we wanted to get married. I started thinking about our future, a wedding, paying off student loans, saving up for a house, children, and retirement. All of a sudden, my staff SLP salary wasn't cutting it. I knew that simply hoping for more money and waiting until I liked my job again wasn't the answer. If I wanted things to get better, I had to make them better. No one was coming to save me. I had to save myself and my family. So I did.

I started my private practice to make a difference in my life, in the lives of my clients, and in my community—but also to help my family. With more financial security, I was able to earn more money in less time, which meant that I gave myself a $24,000 "raise" in my first year of seeing private clients.

Having additional income feels great and takes the pressure off—and I highly recommend it.

I was lucky to have two mentors help me get started in private practice, but then I was on my own.

Back then, there were no courses on starting a private practice. I found a couple of books on mental health private practices and there were a handful of private practice coaches around (all of whom were psychologists—not SLPs.) So, I decided to build a practice and then to share my knowledge and mistakes with other SLPs and OTs to help them succeed more quickly, easily, and affordably. Now I serve as a guide for others, and nothing brings me more joy than seeing the personal, professional, and financial wins that the students in our programs achieve every day.

We're on a mission to help at least a thousand SLPs and OTs build successful private practices each year, because more practices means more services for children and adults who need them. The Private Practice Movement is growing every day. More and more SLPs and OTs are starting private practices in order to help more people while making more money, to have more work–life balance, and to avoid burnout. SLPs and OTs who are part of the Private Practice Movement aren't starting their practices alone. They're starting and growing their private practices with support, in a community of like-minded clinicians who are sick of being overworked, overtired, and underpaid. They're change-makers who aren't just changing the lives of their clients and communities—they're also shaping the future of the SLP and OT professions.

You can join us.

If you need assistance on the private practice journey, I'm happy to help you, just as I've helped thousands of others. There are a lot of steps in starting a private practice, many more than I can include in this book. If reading this book has inspired you to take the next steps on the private practice journey, I'd be honored to be your guide as you start, grow, and scale your private practice.

To learn more about our programs and how we support our students, please visit PrivatePracticeBook.com/Resources or IndependentClinician.com.

This Is Your Time

Trust the timing of your life. There's a reason you read this book. Whether you've been thinking about private practice for a while or it's a recent consideration, you owe it to yourself, your family, and your clients to explore the possibility of private practice.

You don't have to go all in on private practice immediately; you can dip your toe in the waters first by seeing a few clients on the side. This will allow you to build your confidence, your caseload, and your income. It will also help you make sure that you like private practice. If you try it and love it, reduce your caseload at your full-time job or switch to a part-time job while you build your practice. If you try it and you don't like it, you can always return to a school or hospital job. However, I don't think you'll want to go back after you've tasted the freedom, flexibility, and financial independence that private practice offers.

Once you get bitten by the private practice bug . . . you're going to want to continue.

Regardless of what the world may have told you about yourself, you are capable of incredible things.
- You are smart enough.
- You are strong enough.

- You are creative enough.
- You are resilient enough.

You are enough. And you are ready.

Now that you've completed Stage 1: Plan Your Private Practice, you're ready for Stage 2: Start Your Private Practice.

You have so much to give your clients. If you currently work in a school, hospital, early intervention system, or someone else's private practice and you don't feel like you're making a difference because of administrative limitations, you have a choice: Stay in an environment that doesn't serve you or your clients, or create a new environment that serves both you and your clients.

If You Can't Find a Job You Like, Create One That You Love

The Private Practice Movement is for clinicians who want to work outside the box and for clients who want to be served outside the box.

Private practice isn't perfect for everyone, but it's perfect for the right people. The SLP and OT professions need you, your clients need you, your family needs you, and you need you to realize that the pain of being stuck is greater than the discomfort of breaking out of your comfort zone and trying something new. You learned to be a clinician by investing time and money into gaining clinical skills; you're absolutely capable of learning how to be a business owner. You just need to set aside the time and resources to learn from people who have already done it.

Reaching goals requires action. It's not enough to *want* to do something; you have to take steps to actually do it. The good news is, you don't have to start your private practice alone. You can join the Private Practice Movement—the thousands of fellow SLPs and OTs who want more freedom, flexibility, fulfillment, and financial abundance. More and more clinicians are joining us every day.

Some join loudly and proudly at the front; others join quietly in the back. Because so many people are stuck on wait lists and so many clinicians are burning out, *the time is now.* You have a unique opportunity to help more people while helping yourself, too—but you have to act.

You Can Finally Make the Difference You Were Born to Make

You were put on this earth to help people. If you're feeling stifled and stuck in your current setting, unable to make a difference, private practice is the perfect solution.

There are people in every community who are going without services or are stuck on wait lists.

Your future clients are waiting for you to find the courage to start a private practice. Future you is waiting for you to decide that you and your family are worthy of more. You can be a helping-people person *and* a business owner. You can choose to start a private practice on the side and keep your steady pay and benefits, or you can choose to go all in on private practice from the get-go and grow it to your desired level. You can be your own boss and make decisions that serve your clients, yourself, and your family. And you can finally earn what you're worth.

You can be the clinician you've always wanted to be, and you can keep working as an SLP or OT long- term. You can have full control of your life—just like tens of thousands of SLPs and OTs before you, and hopefully hundreds of thousands after you—clinicians who have joined the Private Practice Movement.

You can have a bigger impact.

You can live the life you've imagined.

This is your time.

It's time to start your private practice.

Your Next Steps

Now that you've read *The Path to Private Practice*, here are five next steps to keep the momentum going!

Facebook: Join the SLP and OT Private Practice Beginners Facebook group: PrivatePracticeFBGroup.com.

Instagram: Follow @IndependentClinician and message me to let me know what you thought of the book.

Podcast: Subscribe to the Private Practice Success Stories podcast: PrivatePracticeSuccessStories.com.

Book Bonuses: Log in to get your Book Bonuses: PrivatePracticeBook.com/Resources.

Website: Learn more about Jena and how we help SLPs and OTs: IndependentClinician.com.

Join The Start Your Private Practice Program™: Log in to PrivatePracticeBook.com/Resources for a special link.

Book Bonuses

Included with your purchase of *The Path to Private Practice* are several Book Bonuses:

- Worksheets
- Training videos
- Case study interviews
- Additional resources

The Path to Private Practice walked you through the first stage of your private practice journey, the Plan Your Private Practice stage.

As a former professor, I know the importance of taking action based on what you learn and that many SLPs and OTs are kinesthetic learners who learn by doing.

Utilizing the resources provided as part of your purchase will help you get the most out of this book and set you up for success on the path to private practice.

Visit PrivatePracticeBook.com/Resources to claim your Book Bonuses!

Join The Start Your Private Practice Program™

Start YOUR PRIVATE PRACTICE

Want help implementing everything you learned in this book? We'd love to help you get started! The Start Your Private Practice Program™ helps SLPs and OTs start successful private practices,

step-by-step, so they can have the freedom, flexibility, fulfillment, and financial independence they want and deserve.

The Start Your Private Practice Program™ covers everything from legal matters and marketing to billing and taxes. We'll help you get everything lined up so you can start working with private clients. This program is like the missing course from graduate school, the one that teaches you how to start a speech or occupational therapy private practice. (We even provide continuing education credit!)

Most clinicians don't have the time, energy, or expertise to figure out how to start a business on their own. We've simplified the process and taken the guesswork out of starting a private practice by giving you access to on-demand training videos, checklists, worksheets, and ongoing mentorship. Time is our most precious resource—don't waste your precious time stuck in analysis paralysis. Join The Start Your Private Practice Program™ today.

To learn more about The Start Your Private Practice Program™ and access a special offer for book readers, visit PrivatePractice-Book.com/Resources.

Additional Resources for Every Stage of the Private Practice Journey

The Independent Clinician™ (independentclinician.com) is an online education company founded by Jena Castro-Casbon, MS, CCC-SLP. We teach SLPs and OTs how to start, grow, and scale successful private practices. Our company provides step-by-step advice and ongoing support to help students navigate the private practice journey in the most efficient and profitable way.

Beginner Resources:

- **Free trainings and downloads**: Watch free trainings and download resources to help you plan for private practice at IndependentClinician.com.
- **The Private Practice Success Stories podcast**: Get inspired by the stories of clinicians who have become successful private practitioners. Visit PrivatePracticeBook.com/Resources to listen to our playlist, or search Private Practice Success Stories on any podcast player.
- **Free Private Practice Facebook group**: Find fellow SLP and OT private practitioners who are part of the Private Practice Movement in our free Facebook community: PrivatePracticeFBGroup.com.
- **Private Practice Clinic Forms**: Download 30+ customizable and lawyer-reviewed forms that add a layer of legal protection and take the stress out of starting your SLP or OT private practice: PrivatePracticeForms.com.

- **The Start Your Private Practice Program**™: This is our beginner-level program for SLPs and OTs who want step-by-step help starting a private practice with ongoing support from our team of mentors. Visit PrivatePracticeBook.com/Resources for a special offer for our readers!

Advanced Resources:

- **The Grow Your Private Practice Program**: Ready to go all in and grow your practice? The Grow Your Private Practice Program is for SLP and OT private practitioners who want help with growing their client base, setting up systems, hiring a team, and becoming a CEO. To learn more, please visit GrowYourPrivatePractice.com.

- **The Scale Your Private Practice Program**: Ready to scale your practice to the million-dollar level? The Scale Your Private Practice Program is an advanced program for established private practitioners who want help scaling their income and impact by offering multidisciplinary services, multiple locations, and/or by establishing an education wing in their businesses. To learn more, visit Independent-Clinician.com.

Resources for Undergraduate and Graduate Students:

Are you an undergraduate or graduate student who is eager to start a private practice once you're in the field?

Hello, future private practitioner! I can't wait to help you start your private practice as soon as you're ready. In the meantime, I created a special list of resources for eager students: PrivatePracticeBook.com/Student.

I am also available to speak to undergraduate and graduate classes. If you would like me to speak to your class, school, or alumni event, contact me at: speaking@independentclinician.com.

The Private Practice Success Stories Podcast

Want to hear stories from successful private practitioners?

If so, subscribe to my free podcast, Private Practice Success Stories, to hear how ordinary clinicians are becoming successful private practitioners.

To listen, search your favorite podcast player for "Private Practice Success Stories" or visit <u>PrivatePracticeBook.com/Resources</u> to download our podcast playlist.

Join us each week as we share information, inspiration, and lessons learned on the private practice journey.

Speaking and Media

Jena H. Castro-Casbon, MS, CCC-SLP, is the CEO of the Independent Clinician™. She is the creator of The Start Your Private Practice Program™ and The Grow Your Private Practice Program and the host of the Private Practice Success Stories podcast. She lives in Newton, Massachusetts, with her wife and two children.

She is available for speaking engagements for events, conferences, and undergraduate/graduate level classes. Jena Castro-Casbon's events are designed to inspire, educate, and inform audiences on topics related to private practice, business, and entrepreneurship.

Please contact speaking@independentclinician.com for speaking requests.

Acknowledgments

I would like to acknowledge the following people who have supported me on the journey of life and business.

Dad: You believed in me long before I believed in myself. You taught me to trust my instincts, lead with my values, and use my business as a way to help more people. If not for your mentorship, model, and leadership, I wouldn't be the person I am today. Thank you for your unconditional love and support.

My private practice mentors, Rick Sanders and Kathryn Zainea: Thank you for believing in me and showing me the ropes of starting my private practice. It's because of your generosity in mentoring me that I've committed to a lifetime of mentoring others.

Caitlin Bacher: Thank you for teaching me how to build an online education company, allowing me to grow my impact.

Laura Meyer: Thank you for helping me grow a sustainable business that's focused on creating joy in my life and the lives of others.

The private practitioners mentioned in this book: Thank you to the private practitioners who allowed me to share their stories in this book. Each of you were "regular" clinicians with big dreams. You took control of your professional, personal and financial lives through private practice. You took a chance on yourself (and on me), and it paid off. I hope that the readers are inspired to take action, knowing that your story can become their story:

Bobbi Adams-Brown, Kelsey Martin, Tracy Droege, Olivia Rhoades, Megan Ramirez, Ashtyn Mouton, Marcia Church, Lisa Geary, Ruth Maldonado, Jessie Ginsburg, Claudia Davisson,

Danni Augustine, Katja Piscatelli, Tami Teshima, Sarah Sweeney, Kristin Kudarauskas, Asha LeRay, Glory Lichon, Michelle Eliason, Emily McCullough, Lisa Geary, Dani Gaff, Martha Horrocks, Meera Raval Deters, Christina Bennet, Kristin Beasley, Katie Brown, Adrienne Fuller, Amanda Modrowski, Tia Javier, Rene Robles, Cristina Ramos, and Samantha Asher.

Team Independent Clinician: Carolyn O'Brien Hutwagner: You came into my life at a moment of great uncertainty. I knew that you were the perfect person to help me go from being completely overwhelmed and devoid of systems to having processes in place for sustainable growth. Thank you for taking my business from AHHHHHHHH! to ahhhh . . .

Amanda Aldridge, Bobbi Adams-Brown, Rachel Bakeris, Sarah Breshears, Katie Brown, Claudia Davisson, Michelle Eliason, Adrienne Fuller, Lauren Hermann, Elise Mitchell, Amanda Modrowski, Tami Teshima, and Ben Todys: You are my rocks. You work so hard on behalf of private practitioners and the clients they serve. Thank you for helping the Independent Clinician and thousands of people in our audience #LevelUp!

Elizabeth Sawchak: Thank you for creating the wonderful graphics, quotables, and book website.

My business buddies: Allison Ball, Ebony Green, and Theresa Richard: You've been an extra set of eyes on my business and helped me navigate various twists and turns. I will be forever grateful for your friendship, advice, and confidence.

My family:

Mom: To my bestest pal—You dedicated your life to your family, and I am so lucky that I get to be your daughter. You drop everything to help with everything—especially moves. I love you so much.

Hartley: You're the best sister and friend in the world. We've had some incredible adventures and laughs. Here's to many more. Love, Buffalo.

My grandmother: Audrey Hartley Cahill, (who I call "Muttie"), you inspired me as an author and lifelong learner. I almost took out my middle initial on the cover and throughout the book (because it made my name even longer) but chose to leave it to honor your memory. I wish you could see me now.

Hayes and Holden: I am so proud to be your Mama. You are both so smart and curious. Leave this world in a better place than you found it. Change the world, boys. Know that I will always be in your heart.

Sarah: I knew you were the one from our first day at the CCC. I will always be grateful to you, my partner in life and love, for helping create our wonderful life together and supporting me through it all.

Notes

Introduction

A review of studies conducted across several health care professions identified bureaucratic restrictions, low emotional and intellectual stimulation at work, emotional fatigue, long hours, excessive commitment, and lack of recognition as some of the factors that contribute to burnout in speech pathologists.

Brito-Marcelino A, Oliva-Costa EF, Sarmento SCP, Carvalho AA. "Burnout syndrome in speech- language pathologists and audiologists: a review." *Revista Brasileira Medicina do Trabalho*, 2020;18(2): 217-222, https://doi.org/10.47626/1679-4435-2020-480.

Ilana Kowarski, "What to Know About Typical MBA Courses," *U.S. News & World Report*, June 6, 2019. https://www.usnews.com/education/best-graduate-schools/top-business- schools/articles/2019-06-06/what-business-school-applicants-should-know-about-typical-mba- courses

Chapter 1

"What are the eligibility criteria for students with speech and language disorders?" Disability Rights California, accessed January 23, 2023, https://serr.disabilityrightsca.org/serr-manual/chapter-3- information-on-eligibility-criteria/3-4-what-are-the-eligibility-criteria-for-students-with-speech-and- language-disorders/.

"Speech language pathologist," *Best Jobs* (blog). *U.S. News & World Report*, accessed January 23, 2023, https://money.usnews.com/careers/best-jobs/speech-language-pathologist.

Stamm K, Lin L, and Christidis P. "Psychologists across the career span: Where do they practice?" *Monitor on Psychology*, November 2017;48(10), https://www.apa.org/monitor/2017/11/datapoint#.

Meghan McCarty Carino, "American workers can suffer vacation guilt … if they take vacations at all," *Workplace Culture* (blog), *Marketplace*, July 12, 2019, https://www.marketplace.org/2019/07/12/american-workers-vacation-guilt/

Chapter 2

Reported in the 2015 ASHA SLP Health Care Survey. ASHA annual SLP health care surveys are online at https://www.asha.org/Research/memberdata/Healthcare-Survey/.

Visit https://www.healthcare.gov/ to learn more about purchasing health insurance through the Health Insurance Marketplace®.

Katherine Boyarsky, "How much does it cost to open a coffee shop?" *On the Line* (blog), accessed February 8, 2023, https://pos.toasttab.com/blog/on-the-line/how-much-does-it-cost-to-open-a-coffee-shop.

"Food truck startup costs," *LaunchPointe* (blog), accessed February 8, 2023, https://cardconnect.com/launchpointe/running-a-business/food-truck-startup-costs.

Graham Hoffman, "How much does it cost to open a retail store?" *PosNation* (blog), August 26, 2021, https://www.posnation.com/blog/how-much-does-it-cost-to-open-a-retail-store.

"What is the cost of opening a yoga studio?" *StudioGrowth* (blog), accessed February 8, 2023, https://studiogrowth.com/cost-of-opening-yoga-studio/.

Chapter 3

Brian Hiro, "Speech language clinic goes virtual amid COVID-19" *NewsCenter* (blog), *California State University San Marcos*, August 26, 2020, https://news.csusm.edu/speech-language-clinic-goes-virtual-amid-covid-19/.

Kwok, E.Y.L., Pozniak, K., Cunningham, B., Rosenbaum, P., "Factors influencing the success of telepractice during the COVID-19 pandemic and preferences for post-pandemic services: An interview study with clinicians and parents," *International Journal of Language & Communication Disorders*, (2022)57:6, 1354–1367, https://doi.org/10.1111/1460-6984.12760.

Although malpractice lawsuits are rare for SLPs, they do occur, as this 2006 study shows:

Dennis C. Tanner, "The forensic aspects of dysphagia: Investigating medical malpractice," *The ASHA Leader*, (2006)11:2, https://doi.org/10.1044/leader.FTR5.11022006.16.

Morton, M.E., Gibson-Young, L., and Sandage, M.J., "Framing disparities in access to medical speech-language pathology care in rural Alabama," *American Journal of Speech-Language Pathology*, (2022)31:6, 2847–2860, https://doi.org/10.1044/2022_AJSLP-22-00025.

Rudy Diaz, "The rural challenges of speech therapy," *The Blue Mountain Eagle*, September 18, 2020, https://www.blue-mountaineagle.com/the-rural-challenges-of-speech-therapy/article_233ee1e0-e267-11ea-babb-1ba489df112e.html.

Simonson, J., and Main, K., "Website hosting cost guide 2023," *Forbes Advisor* (blog), updated November 23, 2022, https://www.forbes.com/advisor/business/website-hosting-cost/.

Warren, S., and Nanof, T., "Medicare: A must when treating older patients," *The ASHA Leader*, (2018)23:12, https://doi.org/10.1044/leader.IPP.23122018.40.

Chapter 4

For a detailed description of analysis paralysis, see:

Crystal Raypole, "How to beat 'analysis paralysis' and make all the decisions," *Healthline* (blog), April 27, 2020, https://www.healthline.com/health/mental-health/analysis-paralysis.

As reported in the ASHA 2019 SLP Health Care Survey. The survey is online at https://www.asha.org/Research/memberdata/Healthcare-Survey/.

For more information on SLPs and impostor syndrome, see:

Mattie Murrey, "Overcoming imposter syndrome in speech pathology," *Fresh SLP* (blog), October 26, 2021, https://freshslp.com/overcoming-imposter-syndrome-in-speech-pathology/.

As reported in a survey conducted by SCORE, a nationwide network of business mentors:

"Business mentoring increases start-up and survival rates," *PR Newswire* (blog), May 31, 2018, https://www.prnewswire.com/news-releases/business-mentoring-increases-start-up-and-survival-rates-300657325.html.

About the Author

Jena Castro-Casbon, MS, CCC-SLP, is a private practice consultant, mentor, author, and speaker and founder of the Independent Clinician, an online education company that specializes in helping SLPs and OTs start, grow, and scale successful private practices.

Team Independent Clinician™ is on a mission to help at least a thousand SLPs and OTs start private practices each year, because more practices means more services for the children and adults who need them.

Jena is the creator of The Start Your Private Practice Program™, The Grow Your Private Practice Program, and The Scale Your Private Practice Program, which offer step-by-step information and processes and ongoing support from a team of mentors. When Jena was first getting started, there were no online education programs specifically for SLP and OTs going into private practice, so she created the programs she wished she had.

Jena has been invited to speak at local and national ASHA conferences; she's spoken on starting and growing private practices, marketing, and entrepreneurship.

You can hear Jena every week as host of the Private Practice Success Stories podcast, and you can hang out with her on all social media platforms.

Jena lives in Newton, Massachusetts, with her wife, Sarah, and their two sons, Hayes and Holden. To learn more about Jena, please visit IndependentClinician.com.

Help Me Get This Book into More Hands!

Thank you for reading my book!

As you know, I'm on a mission to help 1,000+ SLPs and OTs start private practices each year, because more practices means more services for children and adults who need them.

There are three ways you can play a role in this mission:

1. Leave a review on Amazon.

Book reviews help books show up in search results and help readers decide if they want to read the book. Please take two minutes to leave a helpful review on Amazon, letting people know what you thought of the book. Here's an easy direct link: PrivatePracticeBook.com/Review.

2. Give a copy to a friend.

If you liked this book and you have a friends or colleagues who might benefit from it, it's a gift that can change lives. This book helps spread the word about our mission to help SLPs and OTs get started in private practice so they can have more freedom, flexibility, and fulfillment and so that children and adults can access the services they need.

3. Invite me to speak to your class, organization, or conference.

I love to share about private practice with undergraduate or graduate students and licensed SLPs and OTs. I'd love to speak at your university, to your state or national organization, or to your conference! Please email speaking@independentclinician.com for speaking requests.

Made in the USA
Columbia, SC
20 March 2023

14065827R00113